Divination and Spirituality of
A SEVENTH BORN
by P. Davies

W0007937

twitter: @seventhborn1

Dedication

I dedicate this book to my wife Jean, a true lover of life, who has taken what she was handed out and faced it square on, not complaining of misfortune or pain, a compassionate and caring person who always kept faith in the human race and guided me back from my dark side with her words of wisdom, a companion whom I was fortunate enough to meet at an early age to fight with me in the low and bad times and to laugh with me in the many funny times, one day we will part our bodies and the pains of living and we shall be reunited in spirit to travel in paradise for all time in the cosmos of our minds.

Contents

Who's Who

1.

You have a gift and must use it wisely

Ever since my first thought and action there had always seemed something necessary for me to do for the benefit of others, and the reason I believe that I am still here is to deliver this message to you all. Being born on the 23 of August 1947, many numerologists will tell you that this is a strange coincidental sequence of numbers that all add up to the number seven, on my seventh birth day my birth mother Elsie, sat me in front of the coal fire, it was a dark winter's evening and the flickering flames cast our long shadows on the walls and wooden floor of our sparse empty living room, the chair Elsie sat herself on, an old wooden spindle-back, and the old pine table surrounded by the four bare walls, were the only witnesses to the prophecy, picking me up and sitting me on her lap, staring deeply into my eyes and lowering her voice to a whisper she said, you are a seventh-born child you have a gift and must use it wisely, be careful of what you do or say in this life, because you will be laughed at and sometimes misunderstood and misjudged, none other than you and I know of your birthright and it must remain our secret for all time, otherwise you may suffer ridicule or even the retribution of others, you will never be poor but you will never be rich in money, but richness comes in other forms of which you will be blessed, you will think differently to others, see things from different perspectives, this will sometimes irritate people because they will not understand and if you are different to them they will fear you and feel threatened, choose all your words through this life well, for they will be words of conviction, you will never want or need, whatever you do in your life good or bad depends entirely on your judgment, turning me towards her staring deep into my eyes she sternly emphasized, don't take this warning lightly, she then placed me gently back on the bare floor by the fire, and from that day never spoke or made mention of it ever again, though over the years she spoke of many other things to do with this special gift. At the time, being only the age of seven it was difficult to comprehend all her words of wisdom, although even at that age I did feel different in some strange way, and it is only now at the time of writing of this book I realise that many of my thoughts and wishes good and bad have turned out to come true but, not being aware of the importance of the message and the warning at that time, it is easy to wish things or curses on people when you don't know the consequences, this we all do at times, but those wishes and curses cast by me were just releases of pressure, and in my defence I would say the real power of the gift was never realized by me until this very moment. Some religions and writings say that seventh-borns can be in league with the devil, some in league with god, some say they are a lycanthrope, some say they can heal, some say they can kill, maybe, but surely that's up to the individual to choose, it is also said that the ancient mariners would conscript a seventh-born child to sail with them on long journeys, he or she was considered a lucky omen and would bring the crew and ship back safely to port even in the wildest raging storms, when one touches the hand or crosses the path of a seventh-born child, the cheat, the liar, the thief will often be exposed and over their years will self-destruct, on the other hand good fortune will prevail to those deserving, but not of the material kind. My belief is that anyone can choose their own path, their own belief, one belief can't curse another if it's not in the believer's head, my thought at an early age was that the seventh-born story was some sort of myth handed down from generation to generation and was just a fairy tale, but after reading my own writings, conviction has entered into my head, so don't discount any possibilities, to me a seventh-born is a wise person given wisdom by experience of life, they are compassionate, honest, faithful and loyal, with truth of word that sometimes can be very cutting, they believe that a spirit-soul, an energy, call it what you will, never dies, yes the body wears out, ceases to function and is discarded but what happens to the energy and the power of those brilliant minds: musicians, philosophers, artists and even just ordinary people like you or me, they still exist, they are here, above you, in front of you, behind you, just waiting to be tapped into. Many people can do this, some unknowingly, have you ever had that intuition, that split moment when things could have been different, a strange presence, a familiar aroma, the feeling that a passed loved one has just kissed you goodbye, a moment of strength when in despair, the strength to carry on when all seems lost, a guardian angel in times of need, that feeling you have been there before? These are not coincidences that many would lead you to believe, and if at this stage of your life you do not relate to any of these things there will come such a time you will. However this book is not all about that, it's about me and my family from the late Forties to the present day and the strange happenings that have paralleled my life, some funny, some sad, some weird, the portrayal of all things in this book are solely my opinion, the opinion of a seventh-born child seen from my point of view, everything is completely true, the characters, some who are dead and some who are living relate to my writing, and many of the names outside the family have been changed to protect the guilty, however all the people in my family have kept their names and they are or were real characters.

So here my words shall be cast, the name of the town and the place of my birth are irrelevant just like my name but a mention won't hurt though this may upset any future mayor of Wolverhampton. In 1947 all towns in England were the same, run down, drab and colourless, still under the shadow of two great wars with a poor standard of living and poverty rife, our generation, the working class, worked for a pittance, with no future except to remain slaves to wealth, but as time passed poor ordinary people stood up and said no, this became the foundation of a Sixties revolution to better ourselves, there amongst the poverty was a spark which one day could ignite into a flame and that flame was to become a glimmer of hope for us all, most people in our area were poor like us and the post-war years were still evident even in the late Forties and early Fifties, ration books were still in use, so the wealthy could distribute food evenly amongst us and we could look up to them and be grateful, the house where we lived was in the heart of the Industrial Midlands and it was a semi-detached property owned by a private landlord, one of a row of five separated by shops to either side, the wonderful thing about it to a kid of my age was we had the air-raid shelter, this stood above ground, one of those thick solid brick ones with a steel door, the interior could hold about ten people at a time and, I should imagine, could stand a blast or two from the payload of a Heinkel or a Dornier, we were situated near some of the main bombing targets during the war, and we were right in the middle of the industrial area, the local factories - Goodyear's, Guy Motors, Guest Keen and Nettlefolds - were on the Luftwaffe's list. This was where the machines of war were made, rusty steel would go into the furnaces then on to the factories where a killing machine of some sort would leave for its destination, that's how efficient the area was and why it was crucial to the war effort, maybe the city has the curse of death over it and this is the reason it never thrived, even to this day being an uneventful place, dull, drab and run down. There's an article somewhere that the town's claim to fame was it had the first traffic lights installed, the lights stuck permanently on red to my mind allowing nothing beneficial to mankind to leave the town, and nothing useful to enter, Jack Manley my next door neighbour used to tell me stories of the Luftwaffe searching the area with incendiaries, which all the locals would put out with sand bags hence the reason every other house had an air-raid shelter. The elderly Mrs Roberts who lived a couple of doors away would stand on her front door step and when I was passing, she would call me over, 'fetch me a bottle of V.P. wine from the chemist sonny', emphasizing a slight cough, she would say, 'it's for my chest', tap-tapping it with her fist, for me to end up crossing the busy main road to fetch her medicine, often avoiding the goose man who would walk his goose-stepping geese to the local butcher for slaughter, it seemed they knew where they were going and they would make one last protest, towering over me and lunging with their beaks in disapproval upon my passing. Returning with the booze, Mrs Roberts would give me sixpence, sit me down and tell me her stories, she used to be stationed on Bushbury Hill during the war, manning the search lights lighting up the sky to guide the anti-aircraft guns to the dark shadows of death that hovered above awaiting the signal to drip chaos on the factories below, in daylight from the top of the hill there was a fantastic panorama, and when you could see through the haze, there spread before you were the beacons of Sedgley and the Wrekin, high points used to warn of troubled times, to the right was Bolton and Paul's the aircraft makers, and further across was the Cemetery where your plot was already awaiting full of past memories of forgotten names and souls, beyond that the Welsh borders, with dirty smoke-stack factory chimneys and foundries in the foreground, this was where the crowds of workers would be called by the factory sirens, just like the Eloi as portrayed in one of my favourite books *The Time Machine*, it was as though the workers were in a trance-like state being called by the Morlocks, walking to their pending doom, this was the area where grey was the colour and black was the future, no was the word, and nothing was the number, and this was where my mother and many others worked making rivets and parts for planes and tanks in the early days of the war, so you see in those times everyone pulled together, unlike nowadays, it seems that the British stiff upper lip has become the British stiff bottom lip, but in times of crisis we the British people can rally and unite if led by the right people, as a child I once read that Napoleon called us a nation of shopkeepers, maybe, but if we catch anyone with their hand in our till, they can look out! Billy Butlin once said, 'give the working class a title and they will work for nothing' how true, if you had a foreman's job or you were a charge hand, you usually wore a bowler hat and a brown apron or cow-gown to show your status and were the only one who could afford a bike, a bike was a kind of statement of wealth to us the lower working class who wore flat caps and travelled by foot, buses cost money and were never on time even in those days, at the factory gates was a clocking-*in* machine you put in your designated card with your name and number to stamp your time of arrival, if you were three minutes late for work the clock card would expose your sin to the foreman and two sins in a week normally resulted in the sack, in reality we were all in the same cauldron so to speak.

The high and mighty neighbours to the right side of us had a large garden and hedge to keep us riff-raff out, they were keen gardeners and they came in very handy as a food source for me and Ron, my elder brother, in our early years, on the left side the people were more down to earth, but not in the gardening sense, not many people with a grafting job had time to spend digging and mowing, when they finished work they wanted to rest from the hard manual work, hence the five gardens to the left were just one open field about one acre square with all the character of the Somme battlefield which made a fabulous secret garden to play in, and often flooded in the winter to create a large lake, and a fabulous place to hide and play, on hot sunny days smoke and dirt from the factories often defused the sunlight and created thick blankets of smog across the town, at times there was a blue haze in front of your face but, when the sun came out, those were wonderful days in the warmth, and often painful when blistering and burning to the skin was the price to pay for chasing coloured elusive butterflies across open fields.

My birth year was one of the coldest on record, transport and industry had come to a standstill for a few months due to the heavy winds and driven snow, on the 23 of August 1947, entering into the food chain through a vortex and into a tunnel with a bright light at the other end there was something pushing me forward, it was an intense force driving me towards the light, with me reluctant to budge, had there been a chance to look into my gene pool it possibly would have been pretty muddy and, had it been possible to hang onto something, there may have been a way to delay the agony of birth and life, suddenly there was a blinding flash with the shadows of faces and outstretched arms and shapes, though welcoming a lost soul, to be pulled out of my cosy warm environment into this cold forbidding place screaming and bawling, and from that time on stranded here in time to fend for myself in this hostile run-down area where, if you don't run with the pack, you are considered odd, and where you are disliked if you are clever and despised if you are a fool. At that moment in time there was no developed brain inside my head to be messed about with so life consisted of lying around in my makeshift bed all day, exposing myself, drinking till sick, throwing things, passing wind whilst throwing my dummy out of my pram and this wonderful angelic girl, W.A.G. for short, would force her breast into my face, take me to bed and always be at my beck and call, often strange women would pick me up and take me out on the town, it was like living the life of a rock star for the first two years, except there was not enough strength in my feeble body to chuck a telly out of the window when having one of my tantrums, but like all wags they have their dummy to keep them happy, and I had mine. Then one day it all ended, the worst thing that could happen, a thought, a developed brain cell, and from that first moment the image of Tommy Davies filled my eyes, my guardian angel whispered in my ear, you are in big trouble.

Tommy Davies was my keeper and master, he was the son of a bargee, him and his family used to ship coal and coffee along the Manchester ship canal by barge, it was a hard job and from a child he lived on the boats with his family like travellers, there were no school lessons for him. he came cast into the profession from birth, born to work, hence the reason Tommy had no education or seemed to have none due to his ignorance of all things, his early lifestyle consisted of shovelling tons of coal or coffee on the barges, transporting it to its destination then shovelling it off again to return to various other destinations, in later years he became a steel moulder in the iron foundries of Netherton near to Dudley, those were hard times and in those days you had to work for your money, he then became a tyre moulder - another grafting job. Tommy was a vile man, completely without style, with a haircut similar to a medieval serf and parting down the middle probably due to the fact pudding basins cost nothing, his ears stuck out like a monkey's and there was a constant stain of snuff beneath his nostrils, he would spit on his hands ceremoniously then rub it in vigorously, especially when about to remove his belt or to commit some misdeed, his clothes were ragged with holes to the elbows of his 'gansey' as he called it, his cheap rubber plimsolls were cut out to allow his bunions and calluses to breath due to the fact that his feet were disfigured by the years of wearing home-made clogs on the barges, he wore gloves with the fingers cut off to keep his meddling nicotine-stained hands warm, he stood about five-foot-six inches small, a thick leather belt around his waist and braces supporting his dirty greasy trousers, that thick leather belt was his weapon to dish out punishment to the innocent, although feeble and thin in stature he ruled with that belt and when a five-year-old is confronted by a giant with a belt the giant usually wins, Tommy had no manners whatsoever, when he ate he did so with his hands picking everything up, he swigged and slurped his tea which he drank from any old jar or container, and his favourite foods were those of poor peasants: whelks and pigs trotters, the whelks were like large sea snails, vile and rubbery, similar to a French *bulott*, and pigs' trotters, sloppy, greasy, and fat similar to a French farmer, he would boil it all together in a pot which would sometimes boil dry to create a vile smell of burning flesh then sit down with his pot of boiled slops, dip his hand in the near scalding mess to pull out the vile concoction to suck the fat and gristle from the bones and shells with the power of a cyclone motor, sometimes causing the meat and flesh to levitate across the two inch gap twixt gob and bone, the grease and bits of flesh flying everywhere, to finish it off by raising the pot and lifting the concoction to his face pouring the remaining greasy slurry down his throat, leaving a shine to his face and hands and dripping on his vest leaving large stains which would be there for as long as he decided, once finished he would leave the sucked bones and swill pot for others to clean then trot off to his pit which was as filthy as him, to sum up Tommy, he had the manners of Charles Lawton's portrayal of Henry the Eighth, the brain of Piltdown Man, and the compassion of Enrich Himmler, he seldom changed his clothes which smelt, and when he washed and shaved which he did on occasion he would splutter and cough phlegm into the sink, leaving the filthy residue for others to clean, and when he spoke it was in a strange tongue a kind of Welsh language mixed with black country, and some of his dialect was difficult to understand, he chain smoked his, 'coffin nails' as he called them and left his fag ash and nub ends to smoulder wherever he chose, sometimes leaving a trail of burned residue behind wherever it lay, when in a bad mood he would walk around on his bare hobbit-feet cursing and muttering to himself in his elvic tongue, and when tired it was a disaster to disturb him from his sleep, once awoken he would come at you in a rage, punching and kicking and hitting with the thick leather belt, sometimes to catch you below the spine which was painful for a few days after, the steel buckle of the belt would sail through the air and come down, destined and determined to destroy all opinion and question, on occasion the buckle gouging a piece of flesh from your leg or back, as he emphasised the blows much like a modern day tennis player would to exert the most force behind their serve, with all his kicks and punches he never hit you on the face so there were no visible scars, this was the punishment for a creaking floorboard, stair or squeaking door hinge, we had to creep around on the bare boards which creaked and groaned with the weight of even the smallest person, he once tried to convince Elsie, my mother, to buy us wooden clogs, they were cheap he said, we would not have minded had they been Clark's but they were the type he would have made himself on the barges and he had to wear as a child, just imagine the noise they would have made, we would have been beaten to death within a week, such was the logic of Tommy. Once the beatings stopped he would for some reason lock me up in a small empty room for two to three days with dry bread and water, Tommy would revel in his sadism and found it amusing. Everything Tommy dished out was turned into a positive by me one way or another and many lessons were learned by me during those internments, which I turned into a kind of meditation that opened up my mind to the truths of this world when confiding with my inner spirit. It was as easy to tell black from white as it was wrong from right, often sitting on the bare boards of that dark drab empty room with two imaginary companions they would duel verbally with each other, parrying each other's questions with an answer, putting their case to me, the bickering would go on for days: who is the stronger, who is the weaker, and who should I side with? Especially as the trophy to the winner would be my soul. In the dark corner was night, and in the light corner was day, black and white fought constantly night and day, neither gained the advantage and neither won, with me only ever coming to one conclusion in my mind: it is a salvation to be brought out of the darkness of your night into the brightness of your day, those lessons gave me time to meditate in the peace and quiet of my situation and born from that time came my great determination in all things, making sure that Tommy never broke me by never showing pain, tears or remorse, deep down inside of my being, even at the young age of five, his was the face of a loser in life, taking his bitterness out of a young defenceless kid. To be disliked or hated one has to earn that position and Tommy earned it, the fear and dislike that burned in my mind was to be the demise of Tommy when in later years his vile life was followed by a vile death, but be warned: what you dish out in this life will come back to you later and tenfold, maybe that's what wise men call karma or is there another reason for it - the retribution of a seventh born.

Due to early influences by advertising boards and tobacco companies telling him how trendy cigarettes were, in all the early movies the film stars always had a fag in their gobs often to portray the cool tough-guy image, Tommy learned to smoke, only to find that later on in life the smoke mixed with the coal dust of the barges, the smelting hot smoke of the foundries and the choking fumes of the rubber tyre industry, his lungs were completely shot, producing green and black phlegm which he spat out at random towards the fire grate or any container that was in the vicinity of his range, often missing and causing a mess, left for me to clean. One of my regular jobs was to get up about six o'clock in the morning before going to school to prepare the fire and clean the ashes from the grate which was often covered with a curtain of thick phlegm that Tommy had created the night before, normally it would drip down the fire grate and overnight would dry a golden brown causing stalactites of crispiness cooked by the heat of the fire, which made me feel sick, matter of fact had he been born today Tommy would probably have been hailed a great grate artist and encouraged to enter his works for the Turner prize, he could have hacked the fire place from the wall, sent it to the Tate Modern and called it his Flemish period, and maybe done a book on Flemish design, except the book would have had to have been kiln dried to stop its pages sticking together, he would have given Tracey Emin and Damien Hirst a run for their money.

Every morning getting up at six was not difficult, there was no pleasure in stopping in bed with Ron and Dave my two brothers they were either fidgeting or piddling it, after leaving the shallow end and then just putting my worn out shoes on and leaving the house in the same damp rags I slept in, it was off to Sammy Lewis's paper shop to get a penny bundle, which was ten or twelve sticks of dry wood tied in a small bundle wrapped with a piece of wire 'and a box of matches please' I would say to Sammy, 'strike a light', Sammy would reply, as he handed them over to me returning my smile with his sunny beam, that smile was inclined to brighten my day until tomorrow, which is probably why he still haunts my memory with a sense of fondness. Returning back to screw up the old *Daily-Herald* newspaper into a ball, lay it on the grid of the grate and stack the small pieces of wood tepee-style, standing on the only chair to get the key off the mantelpiece and collect the coal from the coal house, stack it on the wood and put the key back, not lighting the fire because that was for Tommy to do when he felt cold. Then awaiting for a hush or lull in the atmosphere of the house, crawling under the large table in the corner of the room, hidden by the early morning darkness and out of the sight, keeping deathly quiet whilst awaiting for Tommy to enter the room to light the fire, when he did it was magical, he would stand in front of it and a small glimmer of flame would slowly build to a crescendo, the flashes of heat splashing my cold form when Tommy shuffled from side to side soaking it up, the legs of the table and Tommy's legs partly obscuring the view, and me cowering like a timber wolf in a dark wood glaring from a distance through the trees, mesmerized by this beautiful spectacle glowing in the shadows, after a couple of hours, the temperature beginning to drop, Tommy would leave the room, it was then possible to leave my hide and scramble around the remaining embers curled up like man's best friend, the heat from the floorboards would soon rapidly fade and die leaving the room in near arctic conditions once again.

At eight o'clock it was time to eat and head for school, and after boiling my porridge and gulping it down I set off to walk the couple of miles, the holes in my shoes letting in water when it rained and my clothes worn and tattered, often passing a place called the Cottage Homes where some of the orphans would hang on the railings dripped in finery, clean and smart, waving to me whilst passing, a bit like, the Strawberry Fields John Lennon my favourite musician wrote about, how lucky the kids were in my mind's eye, they were clean, well dressed and looked well fed, and deep inside I longed to go there away from the poverty, however after hearing news programs over the years about the abusing of young kids in those type of places, could personally wring every one of those freaks' necks and of anyone who persecutes young defenceless kids.

One of my many tasks was to take illegal bets into the battle zone, leaving the comparative safety of the Somme I would cross no man's land into the area across the main road called the Scotland's, beyond that invisible line no strangers should cross, upon entering the forbidden area all the roads were named after poets, Wordsworth, Keats, Byron, believe me there was nothing poetic about the place, matter of fact the council were considering knocking the area down and putting up slums, the place was so full of rubbish, old mattresses and scrap metal lying around and paper blowing everywhere, the galvanized-steel silver dustbins tipped up spewing rubbish, the lids which looked like inverted silver shields were never around, they were a useful tool for gathering and sometimes cooking in and, at odd times, to put the hot ash in from the fire grate hence the name ash can, the area was rife with rotting dead animals everywhere, no one ever bothered doing the gardens or cutting the grass, they were happy to live like that, the main problem - this was enemy territory, full of scruffs like me, and they knew every dirty trick in the book, they were scrumpers too, just like me and Ron my brother, trouble was they scrumped money, cars and anything that was available, when you heard a police car bell in the day or night you could bet they were going to Scotland's. Tommy would give me a piece of paper with his bets written on and the money folded inside, it was my job to reach the illegal bookie's house without losing the money or getting mugged, the bookie's was about one mile away in the middle of enemy territory, the gangs of scruffs hung around on the street corners, they could tell a strange face immediately, they would descend upon the intruder like a Scottish defence attacking an English-rugby centre-forward then, forming a scrum with me beneath as the ball, being punched and kicked from post to post an easy target, they would sometimes whack me with sticks, laugh and try to humiliate me and play all sorts of dirty tricks with me putting up with this for years, but they never got the money, always putting it in my sock and they never knew my destination, had their minute pea-sized brains banged on the inside of their tiny Neanderthal sculls they may have had a thought and worked out there was money on me, instead of me going there to get beat up once a week for fun, I read a few years later that one of those persecutors had blown his own brains out in a bout of depression, must have been a bloody good shot, upon reaching the house where the illegal bets were taken heading down the alley dividing the houses, past the cardboard-filled windows, the scrapheap gardens, and the occasional dog cursing me for invading its territory, standing on the back step and banging the filthy door, this Fagin character would appear, tatty gloved hand outstretched, prompting me to hand over the money wrapped up in the paper, he would open it with his grimy exposed finger nails, read it and check the money, 'three tanner cross doubles and a treble' he would mumble to himself, scanning the money, then slamming the door in my face, coming out of the entry and glancing down the street, the spirit of James Cagney my hero whispering in my ear, 'you are a Yankee Doodle Dandy, Yankee Doodle do or die', checking what the going was like, sometimes when it was dry and sunny there was a good to firm chance of getting beat up on the way back because the streets would be full of kids, if it was raining the going would be easy for me the punters never liked a wash, eight furlongs to go to get back home, usually the obstacles were not so difficult to avoid to a young steeple chaser like me who was not carrying any extra weight, having disposed of the money and the burden of responsibility, so, keeping close to the fence at a trot, no one could come inside and bring me down, crossing Poets' Corner and approaching Keats Road, extending to a canter, then clearing a barrier of thick human planks, opening up at Wordsworth, running head down with half a mile to go and heading for the finish at a gallop, hoping not to shed a shoe which often had no laces, two furlongs out, occasionally using the fist to fend off late challengers I probably would have given Red Rum a run for his money, then crossing the finish line with the handicapped well behind me, you see, I was that Yankee-doodle boy and they had usually found someone else to do or die, had the bets failed to get to their destination there would be a steward's enquiry from Tommy and the outcome would have been far worse than anything they could dish out, then hoping that his bets would lose, and most of them did as all gamblers will know, so no return trip was needed to collect any winnings, the way I looked at it, whenever he won I lost, and whenever he lost, I won, therefore winning a lot more times than he was and had the pleasure of seeing his miserable face being pulled as his money went down the drain, so there was another positive

Pete Davies

for me to take from the experience no matter how small.

Elsie May Sutton was my mother's maiden name, her shoulder length hair was always a mess and her makeup slapped on clownishly for convenience, she had no pride in how she looked or lived and all material things were menial and boring to her, she never did any of the tasks a mother was expected to do such as housework, baking or washing, she never got involved, she just ignored all this, and if anyone young or old needed anything you had to do it yourself, 'the lord helps them that helps themselves' she would say with this wry smile on her face, she was an educated woman one could tell by the way she spoke, her accent was different to Tommy's, she had no dialect and spoke clear and straight to the point, blunt but honest, a complete opposite to Tommy, she loved reading, music, and mystical people, fortune tellers and such, she was always talking about ghosts, ghouls, demons and devils, good and bad and the justice that evil-doers can never escape, not the lawful justice but the justice dished out by fate and from the place beyond, this was her belief, in fact if anyone were to imagine a witch, Elsie would fit the profile perfectly though she never said she was, she had been a teacher at an early age amongst other things, she said she taught the piano although we never got to hear her play, when she spoke it was with an air of knowledge, she would tell me stories of retribution that made my hair stand on end, of people who had got their comeuppance, she would call it, for their evil deeds, she spoke of her labours and the cast shadows of imps and goblins dancing around the walls of the sparse bedroom as she screamed in pain at my birth, the hair band that someone had tied around a part of my appendage on the day of my birth restricting the flow, the strange box of bones secreted within a cupboard, imprinting in my mind dread and fear, and at times hoping she was really imagining it all, she spoke of her grandmother who was from the travelling people, the first woman to walk the slack wire one hundred feet above the ground without a safety net, risking life and death, she spoke of the Montgolfier brothers, the first hot-air balloonists, who somehow were relevant to her life, she said she had ties to many people within her family who were mystical people, fortune tellers, seers and such and she believed in them all, she told all her stories in a calming convincing voice that any sage or seer or even a witch would.

Elsie told me we were distant relatives of Jimmy Wild, the championship boxer of the Thirties and Forties, and often told me of the story of his determination, like the determination of a seventh-born, Jimmy was the official world flyweight champion, the class was created in England, his greatest battle was against a fighter named Pancho Villa, a clever hard-hitting tireless and relentless American flyweight who was American champion, the fight ended in the seventh round, a contest that was revered as a classic, the crowd were rooting for Jimmy, 'the Mighty Atom' and the 'Ghost Fighter' they called him, but the speed and skill of Villa could not be matched by Jimmy and from the second round of the contest Jimmy was punched from post to post and went down on the canvass to be saved by the bell, only to continue the rest of the fight under siege, the seconds protested that he had been fouled and most of the ringsiders agreed that the blow had been delivered after the bell had been sounded, in England the American would have been disqualified but this was the U.S.A, however in the third round Jimmy came out of his corner reeling around the ring blinded by the blood from cuts to his eyes but he pressed on, Pancho could pick him off easily, leading blows left and right to the face but Jimmy would not give ground, Jimmy was rocked several times with no failure in his attempts to keep going, seldom was there such a display of endurance seen by a New-York fight crowd, the sheer will and gameness of Jimmy started to convince them that he might have a chance, frail and wobbly though he was, but his end was in sight, his finish was pathetic, he lay face down in the resin beaten to submission. They say as he walked into the last punch he had a smile on his face knowing his demise and accepting his fate, and a right-hand blow from the challenger smashed him to the canvas, the irony was: ten days later the winner of the fight, Villa, dropped down dead, they said it was from blood poisoning from a damaged tooth that Jimmy had handed out to him, or was it the unwritten justice Elsie spoke of, if one could live one's life as honestly to one's self as Jimmy's courage led him to lead his, it would be a fitting life and a fitting end, all these things seemed to tie my mother with the travelling folk, but as the years past she became a broken soul, broken by the disappointment of life and the dismal drab companionship of the person who lived with us, Tommy.

Elsie and Tommy were like the bawdy picture-postcards you see in the shops on Blackpool Sea Front, Elsie was large in stature and Tommy small and weedy by comparison, how they were attracted to each other in the first place is bewildering but as anyone knows, opposites do attract which in this case was very true, Elsie said that when she first met Tommy he looked like George Raft, a good-looking gangster-portraying film star of the Forties, smart in suit and tie and brimmed hat, he must have shrunk a bit since then, and Elsie often compared herself to Mai West, a gangster's-moll-playing actress of the same era, and she must have over inflated over the years, well in any stormy sea or even stormy relationship a Mae West and a raft are perfect companions, but not in this case, they were more like the *Titanic* and an iceberg, destined to meet in a disastrous way, they had both been married previously but were separated from their original partners and I suppose they drifted together by convenience, they just lived together, it probably seemed the obvious thing to come together to survive, in those days it was a sin to shack up with anyone you were not married to, you were an outcast from your family and to all decent people who would judge from their smug ivory towers, probably the reason there were never any pictures or such around the walls of the sparse rooms of the house, nothing to tell of the past of either of them, there must have been some attraction at one time but that had gone, rusted away by time and circumstance only to leave a burnt out shell of an existence, under the same roof, tied together by the responsibilities they had bought into the world, and the one-time flame that had burned for each other had died long ago.

Elsie and Tommy regularly argued over us and occasionally fought each other, often brandishing all sorts of weapons to kill or maim though no blood was ever drawn, the sight of them fighting each other, the kitchen knives flashing in the scuffle, was frightening, often we would cower in the corner of the room screaming and crying, awaiting the final outcome which often ended with a lot of huffing and puffing, like two walruses testing each other, Elsie would grab us together, probably fearing for our safety, and leave the house when Tommy went to work, not intending ever to return, she would walk Ron, Diane and me and the old pram with something in it two or three miles to someone named Freda Alcott, probably the sister of her first husband, we would sit in Freda's scullery while mom talked in a small room at the back of the house, most likely asking for help and advice to solve her situation, 'you have made your bed, now lie on it', was probably the only advice she was ever given. In the scullery one of those old range cookers alight, with pots boiling with the aroma of stews and like and a wonderful warm sofa the three of us would sit on, absorbing the heat from the fire-range, but the ecstasy soon ended and we would end up traipsing back to the hovel we called home, there was nowhere else to go, this would happen often after their battles. Coming back late one night, we entered the house, the living room was aglow with the firelight dancing on the walls, casting the shadow of the chair across the bare boards and bending halfway up the wall, and a lone figure was sitting in the chair in the corner of the room, this grotesque figure was groaning head in hands, upon entering the room the figure revealed itself to the flickering flames from within the grate, its mind and face calloused like that of a leper, I was petrified, thinking one of the many demons my mother had spoken of had come to punish us, my mother switched on the bare, dim, light bulb lighting up the room, it was something vile but human, Tommy Davies, he had had an accident at work and the plasters and bandages had caused an allergic reaction to his skin, all his face was swollen, it took several days for it to pass, there was green and yellow matter and puss weeping from the scabs on his face. Elsie said it was the evil in him.

In my family there are six brothers and three sisters, me being the seventh-born and still not sure who my father is even to this day, hence the violent arguments between Tommy and Elsie. Dave was the youngest, definitely one of Tommy's, so was Valerie, you could see the way Tommy treated them differently from the rest of us, so you can see that Elsie liked to play the field and those are the known ones, Ron and Dianne were definitely brother and sister, so were Geoff, Barry, Arthur, and Joyce, with me a mix of them all. My early school memories are of the left-handed kids who had their hands tied behind their backs, forced to write with the right hand in tears and misery, the ones who could not pronounce words properly were stood over and forced to learn, by punishment, teaching me a valuable lesson that all promises were a waste of time, five miserable years were spent at Woden Avenue Junior school, the main event of my life up to that time was training for weeks to win one of the races on the school Sports Day, the reward was a cricket ball, to me it was a magical prize, just what was needed instead of the potato wrapped in a sock that Ron and I used to play cricket with, which would often crumble with the first blow of the homemade cricket bat which had been ripped out of next door's dilapidated fence which provided a constant supply for bats, on the day of the school sports, winning my race easily, only to find that there were no cricket balls left so had to settle for a hoop and from that day on, at the age of six years, learned never to bother or be fooled with promises ever again and never have even to this day, promises and apologies are hollow, people think that when they apologise for their actions it's okay, why break them or even make them in the first place? From that point on, to me junior school and sport were detestable, not only that, it was the stigma of being poor and seeing the well-dressed kids in all their finery whilst walking around with the arse out of my trousers and the sole of my shoe flapping, when the football team was picked I never had the kit, just a pair of old brown football boots found on the tip with nails where the studs used to be, you had to grease them with dubbin to make them supple to get them on, and they were two sizes too big for me, always last to be picked for the team and usually stuck in goal out of the way, the ball weighed really heavy when wet, and when placed on the goal kick line ready to boot it as hard as possible, the opposition would hover about two foot away, that was the distance it moved in the thick mud after booting it with my matchstick legs, standing there with my Mickey-Mouse physique every time there was a goal kick by me, the opposition scored a goal, the teacher, who was also the ref, would take part in the game as well, if he was on your side you were bound to win, he was the only one able to propel the ball more than two feet but most times it seemed he was on the side of the opposition, once he had the ball it was nigh impossible to take it from him, he would scythe his way through the field, crushing the opposition underfoot purely with his size alone, one time ploughing through the mud towards me with my goal in sight, he fired a thundering shot, and, just like Lord Nelson one of my heroes, for one second taking my eye off the ball for it to smash into my arm, deflecting the ball away from its goal to leave me lying prostrate on the deck in the back of the net in agony, this goliath came running over to me dragging his knuckles along the floor, 'are you okay, well done,' he said, 'yes, Mr Hardy,' I said, 'it's just kismet sir', the word kismet spluttered from my mouth, he then bent over and put a smacker on my cheek, needless to say I avoided all contact sports with philistines from then on, especially where goals were being scored and balls were involved and the ref was batting for the other side, which brings me to cricket, there was a gang of kids who hung out together, they were well dressed and came from the posh part of the area, they were a young brat-pack and the teachers doted on them, 'Harry, pick your team,' the teacher would say, and, 'William, pick yours,' with, of course, me being last to be picked for fear of tarnishing the image of their team, they would all have the flannels, the white pullover, spotless pads and gloves, and me standing out on the field like a scarecrow at a fashion show, ragged-arsed on the crease, bat in hand with mud on my wellies and a button missing off my donkey jacket, lastly the barn-dancing class, boys sitting on one side of the room, girls on the other, 'choose your partners,' the teacher would shout, with me as usual left till last, the class male scruff to be partnered with the equivalent female scruff, only her being two stone bigger than me and smelling of mothballs and Dreft and looking like a Bond villain, the teacher would glare at me so, crossing the room sheepishly, to be grabbed like a rag doll, my partner dressed like Rosa Klebb in the film *From Russia with Love*, her two-piece grey suit and tie designed by the K.G.B. at the Kremlin, both of us dancing together like Bond and Klebb, fighting to avoid the deadly poison knives embedded in her shoes and holding each other in a judo stance to the sound of Dosey Doe, with her dance moves similar to sumo wrestling, leaving me twisted and distorted and out of shape and needing a bed at the A. & E. at New Cross Hospital.

Days later, whilst walking home down Woden Avenue alone and totally unarmed except for my crutches, there before me was a glistening in the grass about ten yards ahead on the roadside verge, upon approaching the glinting glow, it looked like a silver cross, getting nearer it changed and manifested into a sword, why had no one noticed it? It stood upright, point of blade dipped into the earth, swaying in the breeze as though marking the spot where some great battle had been fought, on hindsight could it have been marking the lost battlefield searched for by many local historians and mentioned in the *Doomsday Book* when the Anglo Saxons routed the Danes in Wodensfield over a thousand years ago? or had some ghost of some great warrior from the past left it there for me to fight in battles to come? That sword was something special to me, thinking, how could anyone leave this here?' it was the most wonderful thing ever, on many occasions trying to make swords for my imaginary battles against evil, but being no great mysterious samurai sword-maker, my wooden swords often disintegrated after the second blow, now, there before me, lay the greatest sword ever, it was the sort a saint would wield, the wide metal blade shone in the sunlight and the hilt and pommel were in the shape of a cross with the handle wrapped with leather and fabulously bejewelled, probably with glass, like a great king picking it up, raising it above my head, 'Harry for England and Saint George,' echoed through my head, the sword was light and could be wielded easily by my feeble sword arm, panicking with ecstasy and anticipation and taking the sword back to my dark dungeon of a bedroom, hiding it under my bed, smouldering with the joy and glee of my find for days, not daring to reveal it to the world, then one day finding the courage to hold the sword once more, taking it out into the sunlight and the security of the garden to become the finest and greatest swordsman that walked the earth, as the days passed it became less likely that the owner of the sword would appear, carrying it everywhere, cleaning it, owning it with pride, then David, my youngest brother and Tommy's favourite, challenged me and tried to take my precious from me, fighting him off defending the honour of my sword, the mêlée attracted the attention of Tommy the troll, who disarmed me with one blow to the back of the neck, knocking me to the ground, he took my sword and in front of my eyes carried it to the worn doorstep where many blades had been honed and ended their lives, placed it across the sacrificial step and jumped on it in a troll-like fashion, snapping it in half, destroying my sword, my demon-slayer, my cross of justice and breaking my heart, it was never to be seen again, how could anyone be so mean as to take pleasure in destroying such beauty? maybe he just did not like crosses, crying and sulking for days alone, inside me the dislike for Tommy grew more and more, and also a dislike for the little weed Elsie had spawned who ran to Tommy and told him of all the goings-on of the day, David was his favourite and he was obviously the seed of Tommy, he had his mannerisms and stature even at that age of four, but all those treacherous traits became of no use to Dave in later months because the path that life took him on was that of misery, a few weeks later one of Tommy's pots of gruel sat simmering on the stove unguarded by Tommy, in his ignorance poor Dave reached up to the handle and pulled the cauldron of filth towards himself, immersing his form in boiling swill, and from that day on Dave suffered a thousand agonies being transported back and forth to hospitals to have large pieces of skin cut from various parts of his body and grafted to the damaged areas, the scars and the burns to his torso were in the shape of a tree, to see the Tree of Lebanon often reminds me of poor Dave, any such victim nowadays would not have survived the shock, this not only forged the future for Dave in his stature but also made him lose most of his sight, at the age of six he became a weak thin little chap with a head that wobbled to and fro to focus himself, and he could not see above three feet in front of him, for this he became the brunt of normal persons to mock and make fun of because he was different, and all his years he has been ridiculed by persons more fortunate than him and of normal stature and even to this day we would defend him in a confrontation and it was often the case when he was growing up as a child, you see, it was only his body that was scared not his brain but no one saw this, they saw the body of a fool and treated him so, through his school years even the teachers had no compassion, Sam the maths teacher would whistle as he spoke, calling

---

Dave a 'sssssstupid boy,' 'go for the cane,' was his catch phrase, because of his lack of sight Dave could hardly see the blackboard so had to memorize everything he was taught, obviously his grades were not as good as others so the teachers often sent him for the cane for bad work and not concentrating, he eventually ended up in lower classes amongst the ones who did not want to learn, nowadays he would have gone to a special school for help with his disability but in those days you were thrown into the same mix, but the reputation of Ron gave Dave a cloak to shelter under from the bullies, they would be answerable to us, it was them who were the fools, how they judged and took advantage of lesser fortunate persons. When Dave became old enough to leave school he had to go to work classed as an able-bodied person, someone took him on as a floor tiler - his work could not involve machinery of any kind. There are certain trades and persons that one has to be aware of in this life and the building trade is no exception, it is rife with con men, liars and cheats, ask most of them how long they have been in the trade, and they will answer 'what time is it?' I have met most of them, being in the trade myself for forty years, and Dave has been a victim of them all, he has been robbed and stolen from all of his life because he could not see and was an easy target, even when Tommy, in his will and after his death, left Dave the house to live in which none of us contested because it was a chance for him to live some sort of life without worry, some female parasite with delusions of grandeur latched onto him and persuaded him to sell the house to buy a bigger one for her gain, needless to say Dave could not resist the sex or afford the mortgage the bank gave him, he was unemployed at the time, they obviously smelt the £25,000 pounds he had from the sale of the family home, eventually he lost everything to be homeless for a while, sometime later he told Jean, my wife, of his plight and she managed to get him some disability allowance for his sight and he applied for a council flat, one of those failures of the Sixties, you know the ones, the high-rise designed for a better future that are now ghettoes for every failure in this life, we visit him on occasion, talking to him one day in his flat, a commotion and banging came at the door, 'police open up,' came a voice through the letter box, 'if you don't open up now it's a two thousand pound fine,' panicking, Dave went to the door to be confronted by the Drug Squad barging past and chasing a suspect, they ran through the flat to the balcony and there below was this fool climbing down the outside of the building jumping from balcony to balcony, it was so high and I was looking over the balcony at the idiot and glancing past him towards the ground just to make sure my car, which was a small dot from that height, was not directly below and going to be his coffin, and imagining the mess he would make of the paintwork if he fell on it, to the side of my car there was a half a crown glinting on the pavement far below, sheepishly taking my leave and feverishly going for the lift, which was broken, dashing down the filthy stairs all twenty flights eventually reaching the bottom clutching my chest and gasping for air, almost doubled up with the stitch, staggering outside to find it was one of them damned silver dustbin lids, ah well, such is life, never attempted the journey back, would have needed an iron lung. To this day, Dave lives his life as a hermit away from mankind, he does not fear them, he just can't be bothered to be part of them, to him it's a burden to meet any person, he always expects the worst, locking himself away in his tower hamlet far above the crowds in his Quasimodic lifestyle, looking down from his balcony, watching the once-vile mocking ant-like creatures far below, trouble is there is no Esmeralda and no happy ending for Dave, only the burden of the scars and the curse that fate handed out to him. The one thing that keeps him sane is his love of music and the Bee Gees, the late Robin Gibb reminds me of Dave, they were spitting images of each other, he learned himself to play the guitar and can sing quite well, and Robin wasn't too bad either, the last time we met Dave seemed a bit depressed and, unlike him, he was concerned about how he would meet his end, no matter how he leaves this place it will be easy for him because there has never been any peace here, the burden that he has carried through this life would be the end of many a lesser person and he can look this place square on, knowing full well he is special and, when death does come, Dave, if you ever need a guide to the next life, wait for me in spirit as I will for you.

What is that elusive thing that keeps us going in times of depression? Some of us can ride the storms of life, others just collapse and give up at the first sign, why does the will to live disappear in certain persons whilst others carry on? Are you searching for the answer? You may say, 'the answer to what?' Well, the reason to be, to exist, there has to be a reason doesn't there otherwise what's the point? My mind is getting confused, the repetitive nature of being reoccurs and one can only see this with the onset of age when dreams and aspirations start to dissolve into fantasy born from an early age, saddened to see regression, there is something, but at this time is it possible to put my finger on it? No, but believe me, I will. Life is like a puzzle that each individual has to work out only many don't see it, some can complete the puzzle and find contentment, others won't even look at it, and some try to do it and fail, I'm still trying to work mine out, but sometimes the pieces don't fit and my picture is different, people are like pieces of a puzzle needing to fit in together, the trouble with me is I don't feel part of their puzzle, and have got my own to work out, it is unacceptable to me that we are here to work then die, ready to face the wonderful place beyond, of which we are told of by persons who have never been there, neither will my mind to be fogged by the acceptance of a pointless death, somewhere is the key to my being, we are all passing visitors to this planet, our dust will drift back out into the cosmos after a few years, maybe to wonder through time or just feed the planet as all deceased do, but for a brief moment in time we do exist and, when you exist, you must believe or have a belief to give you reason to be, once you lose your way, your life passes by wastefully, till eventually most people just give up and rot away in the chains they have forged for themselves, to live your dream you must have a dream, but make sure you have a dream that you can see, don't listen to the losers who will tell you it's impossible, you can do it, it's easy, ignore that brainwashing box in the corner of the room run by the advertising companies, it's full of fools and they will only depress you, and, let's face it, who in their right mind would buy double glazing off a lunatic whether they get one free or not? There are all kinds of idiots on there telling you that you can win fabulous amounts of money with stupid questions and everything will be wonderful, they are only lining their own pockets, the other day some bloke was commenting on the cut and style of women's dresses and how lovely their expensive Charlie-Chan shoes were, well whoever! no man is interested in women's attire unless they wear them themselves, for a man to say a woman's dress is beautiful is like a woman explaining how a carburettor works or the off-side trap, in the main it just don't happen, it's all just fantasy, it makes you imagine you can be like they portray, happy and living a wonderful life, those chefs' programs, they are so boring, they tell you that it is possible to cook an omelette in twenty seconds, to stand over them and make them eat every bit is one of my greatest desires, suppose these feelings stem back to when hungry as a child, idiots playing games with food when there are so many starving in this world, wastrels Elsie would call them, wasting good food just for gratification, and those reality programs where they eat all sorts of insects for money, isn't that cruelty - just because they are ugly, the insects that is, but that's just another context, so just ignore them all, they are fools to themselves and liars to you, watering the truth so it's bearable, in effect, they tell you to live a lie. Make a decision and stick to it, don't let anyone get in your way, ignore common sense, there's no such thing if you want to live your dream, all those things you want to do and are told that you can't, well so do those who criticise but just don't have the courage to carry it out. Remember the time we visited Freda Alcott and there was something in the old coal pram? well that was Valerie, she was the second youngest and my youngest sister, a person with no dreams or even the chance to dream, you see she was a spastic, nowadays in today's society it's not ethical call her that but that's what she was called all her life, she was born one year after David on Saint Valentine's day, hence the name, Elsie said she fell off a chair whilst getting a pot off a shelf which brought on the premature birth, more like she tried to get rid of her due to the fact she was another of Tommy's, though later Ron told me that Val's umbilical cord got wrapped around her throat during birth resulting in oxygen starvation to her brain, Valerie was fat and overweight, she could hardly walk and had the mind of a three-year-old, Elsie had a full time job looking after her and she did not get any help from a social-services system like one would nowadays, and earlier when I spoke of the unconditional love of a mother, well, that love showed in Elsie for Val, Val needed her constantly and Elsie was always strong, she would protect Val and defend her even when Val stabbed her or attacked her in one of her uncontrollable rages, Mother/Elsie would turn her eyes away when disagreement set in and, in the times of Val's depression, she would pick herself up mentally, and run to Val every time she called, that's the love of a mother and that's the compassion and determination I saw and inherited from Mom. Valerie went to special school every day, picked up by a coach in the mornings and dropped off at night, she loved doing jigsaws and should anyone try to fit a piece she would become violent, lashing out at anyone with the strength of ten men, even to this day the temptation to pick up a piece of a jigsaw and slot it in place is avoided by me in memory of the wrath of Val, it was difficult to control her when she was angry and best not to say too much to her for fear of upsetting her and getting injured, should she have knife or fork or any weapon she would try to stab you with it and, if she was unarmed, her favourite form of defence when anyone upset her was what Ron and I named the 'death grip' after suffering many of her pincer movements, she had this knack of gripping you under the upper arm, on the fleshy part when you weren't looking, and pinching with an unbelievable strength which would bring you to your knees slapping the canvass like a wrestler, the pain would be excruciating and the only way to stop her was to twist her arm to break her grip, then she would start crying and tell Elsie or Tommy you had hit her, thus resulting in another beating from the other spastic in the family, Tommy, the bruise under your arm would be there for about a week and very painful, it would have bought Jackie Pallow to his knees which is probably where she got it from, she loved to watch the wrestling with Tommy on a Saturday afternoon on the television, one day she complained of a pain to her leg, Elsie took her to the doctors who said it was nothing, the next day she was dead. It was a blood clot and it travelled to her heart, it was a blessing to Elsie, who had truly looked after Val for thirty years with no help from anyone, the thing about Val was she had no education of any kind and she was interested only in things that happened at the time that passed through her goldfish memory, she could not read or write, and in her last hours in this life, Elsie told me that Val spoke of a man in the clouds calling to her, she said he was in a white suit, Val was not capable of making up such a story she never

Pete Davies

knew of, or understood gods or angels, Maybe it was an angel, or maybe it was the spirit of Jackie Pallow about to ask her if she would like to form a tag team, who knows. You may think I am flippant about this and should show sorrow, my tears were shed for days after her death, there were tears for Val and the miserable existence she had, also there were tears of joy that she had discarded that useless form and gone on to where her mind and spirit took her, after living in the same house as Val for twenty years, it was difficult then to understand and justify why a person like Val should have to grow up in a world so harsh, to have to struggle through a meaningless existence just to eat, sleep and die, when we able-bodied have a choice of some sort but usually waste the time we have here.

Now to my favourite brother, Ron, the one most of my childhood was spent with, he was a year and a half older than me born on the 21st May 1946 he must have been bored waiting for me to arrive, from the day we blacked each other's eyes we were good friends, we forged a bond and were inseparable for many years, Ron was a chubby-faced lad with curly hair which hung down like a Jacobean prince which was strange, no one else in the family had hair like that, matter of fact Ron, Dianne and Dave had a full heads of hair in later years, but me, the same as my half-brothers, just one giant parting. They all had weak eyesight, Ron had to wear national-health glasses, the type John Lennon wore in later years, they were classed as poor people's glasses in the Fifties, funny how trends can change. Together Ron and I educated ourselves at the rubbish tip which was about a mile away - there was no literature of any kind in the house, only Tommy's racing paper, *the Daily Herald*, we would walk to the tip which was about a mile away, it was a huge hole which had been excavated after the war to become a sand and gravel quarry, then to become a rubbish tip, the size was emphasized because it was on a hill, the same hill that housed the anti-aircraft guns during the war, when we reached the edge we would slide down the tip bank on a piece of corrugated sheeting to be ejected into the pile of rubbish, sifting through it for hours, it was a goldmine of books, postcards and all sorts of Twenties art-nouveaux figurines, probably worth a fortune nowadays, if Time Team were to excavate the area they would find wonderful relics of bygone days and probably loads of coins and jewellery but, being naïve, we thought at that time such things were just junk, and now they are compared to literature and knowledge, this was where we discovered our first books, Jules Verne and Dickens, Conan Doyle, Churchill, we loved science fiction and the Sherlock homes mysteries and books about the war, we would collect the ones we wanted, clean them off, cart them back to the air-raid shelter and stack them to read in peace and quiet at a later time. On summer days, if you sat on the dirt floor behind the air-raid shelter, you could catch the early-morning sunlight and be washed by its warmth and be away from the eyes of Tommy to get some peace and quiet to read, there was a book shop in Hoarsely Field just outside Wolverhampton where you could exchange comics and books, this is when my love for art and drawing started.

Our main task was survival, to be able to feed ourselves, the food Elsie supplied was like gruel and there was not much anyway, so we would kit ourselves out and at night travel to the right, across the fenced gardens of the posh and educated, the ones with office jobs for whom, after sitting down all day immobile, gardening was a release from the drudge of office walls, it was no good going left, they were all paupers and lower working class and the only thing they ever grew was tired, we would often go at night, causing mayhem, treading on cloches and walking into glass greenhouses, when the moon shone was the best time, there was less chance of injury, the only problem was that we were visible to the enemy and if we were caught we would have the wrath of Tommy to contend with, so we would eat the apples and pears as we went and the monochrome light of the scrumpers' moon made them look perfect, if we got caught at least it was on a full stomach, we also had a poacher's bag which we would fill for the next day. When we saw our spoils in daylight and Technicolor they were full of grubs and things, to us it was just more nutrients, one particular night my bag was loaded with booty, I stumbled and fell over, got up and sticking out of the side of my knee was a broken Bonn-coffee bottle, remember the ones, square in shape like a sauce bottle with a liquid chicory coffee-tasting liqueur in them? It was about three inches long and the neck and the cap was still on it, there was a darkness to my skin in the moonlight, feeling a stickiness to my leg and pulling the bottle neck out of my knee, it never hurt at first hence giving me the courage to do so, after about a minute or so the throbbing pain started and the blood was gushing to leave me howling at the moon, Ron helped me limp back across the gardens and we managed to get some rag to stem the bleeding but as soon as it was removed it started again,

Ron got a piece of clean newspaper, chewed it in a ball and pressed it into the wound, he was smart like that and he could always solve a problem, probably saw Tonto do it in a Lone-Ranger film at the local flea pit on a Saturday morning but it worked, the blood slowed to a trickle, then tying a piece of clean rag around it, not daring to mention it to Tommy or Elsie, in those days if you fell or injured yourself they used to clout you around the head and accuse you of being stupid, therefore limping for about three months, changing the make-do bandage in secret when the blood shone through and never mentioning a word of it to anyone and, if questioned, 'just fell over', would be the reply, or, fell off my crank of a bike, salvaged from the tip which had no tyres, brakes or pedals therefore often grazing my knees on the coke ash they used to lay down on the verges around the shops, eventually it healed but the scars are still there to this day which sometimes hurt in cold weathers. The neighbours to the left of us were the Manley's, Jack Manley was a self-employed builder, his mannerisms were calm, collected and logical, we used to help Jack with odd jobs he was a kind of father figure and he would pay us in some way or another, sometimes with a couple of bob and other times with the use of his workshop in which he had all sorts of machinery, Doug and Allen, his two sons, used to do fretwork and many of my days and weeks were spent learning their skills, Jack was also a very skilful man, unlike Tommy who had no skill whatsoever, Tommy used to say he had great footballing skill, he certainly had a footballer's brain because he used to dribble a lot, he said that when younger he had a trial for Manchester United, they played him at right back, after the trial that's where they sent him, right back from whence he came, they were going to play him in goal as a last resort but, remember, he didn't like to handle crosses(sorry just couldn't resist it).

In later years Alan crashed his van into a lamp post killing his young daughter and his wife on impact, when the fire brigade came, his legs were trapped mangled in the wreckage, they said they could not save his legs and a surgeon came to cut them off, Alan grabbed the surgeon by the neck, threatened him and, needless to say, they cut the metal away instead, after two years on crutches he was able to walk again, how about that for determination? In later years Jack divorced his wife for having an affair, the bloke wasn't even half the man Jack was - or maybe he was and that was the attraction to Dolly his wife - she went to court for a divorce and got half the house and that left Jack a broken man to live and die alone sometime after, but good does get its reward and Jack was a good man, for good men and the memories of good men never die, he taught me a lot of building skills and art, and skill and art live forever like happy memories, unknown to me at the time, those were Jack's gifts to get me through my working life.

The other side of the house were the Holders', they had white-collar jobs, and compared to us they were well bred, old man Holder had an immaculate vegetable garden, everything one could dream to eat he grew there, he had a huge glasshouse at the bottom of his garden loaded with temptatious foods, bright coloured fruits grew in abundance but it was forbidden land for us paupers. The Holders' garden was surrounded by a large privet hedge about six feet high reinforced with barbed wire and it was guarded like the Berlin Wall, they would patrol it every so often looking for holes and would repair them to keep us out, but no matter how hard old man Holder tried to protect his veg we concocted all sorts of contraptions in Jack's workshop to obtain it, there were designs everywhere like the contraptions Leonardo would draw, ripped out of books that Ron and I had discovered at the tip we just modified them, there was even a drawing of a helicopter in that book that we back engineered into a potato peeler, but we never got round to making it, we could lasso lettuces and pinch the peapods with great ease, we even made this concertina grab with a claw on the end to rob the rhubarb and with a bag of sugar spent most of the day gorging ourselves on the fruits of his labour, only to be groaning in agony with stomach ache for days after, once eating a two-pound bag of sugar and about ten sticks of rhubarb to have diarrhoea and worms for a week. They had two sons. John and Tony, John seemed odd to me, he wore lipstick and plucked his eyebrows and put eyeliner on and he dressed in flamboyant frilly clothes like a woman which was a strange thing in those times to a seven year old to comprehend, if our football happened to go over their garden John would dash out of the house stab it with a knife frantically, like that woman in that Alfred Hitchcock film, laughing insanely and plunging the knife in repetitively, he would then throw it back over the hedge deflated like our egos, if our spud in a sock went over he never threw it back, suppose he made some chips with them, we could just imagine him calmed down, giggling insanely to himself as he diced up the spuds, we did not mind, the spuds was theirs. maybe he was practicing for when he grew up to be some sort of psycho, judging him by his actions, they were so petty, promising myself, no matter what happened in my life, never to be so miserable or weird as him, oddly enough in later years he took his own life according to the police report and the headlines of the local paper, he had parked his car in a country lane down the road from the house and drank a cup of industrial cyanide which burnt most of his head away, wonder why he did that, there are easier ways to kill yourself, proved my point, he must have been mentally unstable to do such a thing. Had I unknowingly cursed him to such a vile death? For many years after the question burned in my mind, the dread and fear of reprisal for those actions to a young lad like me influenced by his mother's preaching was dire, but my conscience is clear, after reading these words it's plain to see that I never disliked or wished anything on him, just found him odd. One afternoon, sitting at the bottom of the garden cooking some veg in our homemade billycan, something came flying over the Berlin Wall, upon investigation it was a small mole, they had bashed it with a spade and chucked it over the hedge, think what they would have done to me or Ron had they caught us, we picked up the moley little soul and slowly nursed him back to health, we named him Pete because he loved to practice digging in compost, we were going to call him Gordon, after Flash our hero, that's how he appeared, in a flash, flying through the air, come to think of it he always had a greasy grin on his little moley face similar to the one that some modern day politicians have when lying to the public, and he had that same little grin especially when he was about to go next door to do some digging, we would give him one egg a day and some free vegetables (of course!) and a stick of rhubarb to strengthen his little paws, we knew he loved archaeology because he used to create all sorts of burial mounds on the Holders' lawn, he carved out the Malvern Hills once and Sugarloaf Mountain, ah! One day he never returned for his supper, Tony must have blown him up with a mole bomb. Ron and I thought of writing a letter to the government in protest, we read that there were many moles working there and in MI5, which we thought was the abbreviation for Mole Investigations for five-year-olds, then, after we read the Daily-Herald headlines - that most of the moles had left and defected to Russia - we decided to write to the Queen to see if she could form some kind of mole medal for the New Year's Honours List for those that had survived, she could call the medal an M.B.E. 'Mole Bomb Escapee' or she could even help form a Mole Veterans Society because many suffered from mole-bomb fatigue, after all it was Churchill who coined the phrase, dig for victory, and Pete was only doing his bit for his country.

The path you take in life is somehow cloned with the one your parents follow, the male for the male, the female for the female, that's my observation, take Dianne for instance, she was intelligent and not bad looking but she had the same fate as Elsie, her life was a total waste, she met this bloke, got married, had a couple of affairs, got divorced and died alone from a heart attack at the age of fifty-four, can't say much about Dianne, she was a girl and in those days they did their thing and lads did theirs, when Dianne was a teenager, about thirteen, she brought a friend home from school and this girl wanted to stop the night, which was strange because our house was filthy and what sort of person would want to stay in a place like that if they had a choice? Anyway, Elsie said she could, halfway through the night Dianne started screaming and Valerie was crying, all three had slept in the same bedroom and they had seen this demonic face at the window which was frightening especially as the bedroom was upstairs, this caused a commotion and Tommy was not happy, 'yom all mawkins', he snarled, which was one of his misinterpreted colloquialistic malapropisms, really it's Welsh for 'stupid', he trundled back to his pit mumbling and tut-tut-tutting, 'don't wake me again old buggers', he shouted as he slammed his bedroom door behind him, mind you there was some credibility in their screams, Ron, Dave and I slept in the bedroom next door and the cupboard doors in our room started banging violently, at about the same time a dark crouching spindly impish shadow crossed the window and we shouted and screamed affrightedly irrespective of the warning from Tommy, the mêlée awoke Elsie who came into the room and the banging of the doors stopped and the shadow had gone, but when she left the room it started again, we never slept and spent all night in fear, listening to the groaning and banging of the doors, next day just before this girl left the house she turned to my mother and said, earlier this morning this awful urge came over me to push your Val down the stairs, Elsie went berserk and chucked her out, Dianne found out a few weeks later that this girl had been stealing from the local church she had apparently blasphemed the altar and the vicar had thrown her out, calling her an evil person, sounds odd that an evil person would admit to it, maybe she was evil and vile and was proud of it, come to think of it, I have no faith in any isms at all, believing in the power of will, the energy of the earth and the universe, our true mother from where we come from and eventually we all go back to, many do not believe this, to me most people are too blind to see or feel the energy that comes from within one's self, it's easy to imagine people laughing at me now, the same way each religion laughs at each other and their estranged gods, what's the point in worshipping gods who only concern themselves with the fates and actions of human beings? To people who are questioning and searching, rethink your position, wash your mind of all the things you have been told from an early age, seek for yourselves, you can't lose what you haven't got can you?. After the cupboard door incident few months later, there was another noise in the bedroom, we had been watching *The Quatermass Experiment* on the telly at Jack's house with Doug and Allen, the one set in the Fifties about a spaceship, when the Things walk through walls, we were absolutely petrified, not only that, spaceships and aliens were the in thing at the time, promoted by the American film industry, they were always advertising on bill boards about the coming invasion, one of Ron's favourites was a film called *The Invasion of the Body Snatchers* it was about aliens coming to earth, growing a pod near your house or in a greenhouse, waiting for you to die naturally or by accident, then replacing your body with a living alien clone set to dominate the world, and also we had read *War of the Worlds* a couple of days before, fuelling our fears, we had gone to bed about nine as we did every night when, in the middle of the night, alone in our bedroom, the curtain started to shake and move on its own, Elsie came in answer to our repetitive screams of, 'the curtain's moving!' she turned on the light, nothing, 'now shut up you lot, if you wake Tommy you will be for it,' she said and left agitated, five minutes later the curtain started to move again, under the army coat on the bed the three of us were sweating with fear even though the inside of the window was covered in frost, Ron said he was going to get out of bed and turn the light on, boy was he brave, sure enough he got out of bed, turned the light on, nothing, the curtain had stopped moving, 'right,' said Ron, 'give me the army coat', it was freezing cold, he wrapped it round himself and whispered, he would wait by the light switch and if anything happened turn the light on so we had to keep our eyes on the direction of the movement, after a few moments the curtain started again, on went the light in just enough time to see a little mouse run down the curtain and into the back of the old redundant fire place, whew what a relief, we looked after him, fed him with peas and scraps of food for months till he disappeared, Elsie's food probably killed him, the mouse that is, not Ron, or maybe the little mouse refused to eat and starved to death. There is a moral to this little mouse story: fear and imagination fuelled by confusion are created in your own head and most times magnified by odd circumstances, which is the way some evils are created, some of it based on fear, some of it on hearsay, and some of it dreamed up by absolute nutcases. In my belief there is none of this ugliness, my life is based on logic and common sense with just myself to answer to and if you search deep enough you will always find the truth.

In the early Fifties black people started to come to England to earn money, it was in 1952 at the age of five, whilst sitting in the dust by the main road playing with my whip and top, the equivalent to today's play station, the thing was you could make a whip out of a piece of wood and an old leather boot lace and a top from one of the Saxon pop bottles that had stone stoppers, it was a sunny day and I was happily whipping away when suddenly it went dark, there towering above me in his dapper suit and wide brimmed hat stood a man with black face and hands, he was about to walk past but he abruptly stopped as though distracted, he put his large brown suitcase down in front of me blocking the rest of the world from my view, he must have asked me something, he was bending over me directly in front of me, he cast a giant shadow exaggerating his huge black figure silhouetted by the sun, with me squinting, the sun in my eyes, and thinking it was Daniel's the coal man on his rounds, my pupils dilated and became accustomed thus clearing my vision, the sight put the fear of all fears in me, it was the Bogey Man, I ran screaming into the air-raid shelter, that was the nearest escape, leaving my whip in the dirt and my top where it spun, once inside, cowering in the corner behind the books, awaiting for him to show his face and put me in his case and take me away to Robertson's, never to be seen again, sitting in the dark for hours too frightened to come out, to eventually brave the sunlight and find he had gone, never said anything to Ron, cowardice was frowned upon by both of us and looked upon as a weakness. We had just finished reading *The Four Feathers* two days previous, another one of our tip finds. To be likened to Harry Faversham, the coward in that book, would have brought shame on me; to be seen as a gung-ho hero like Dan Dare, defeating the evil Mekon, or even Flash Gordon forever challenging Ming, those where my role models, my heroes. Though in hindsight, in today's society amongst the black country working classes, tell someone that you would like to be like Flash, or even Danny Dare, they would give you queer looks, come to think of it many of the phrases from my youth have become camp and smutty, when you were gay you were carefree, and camp was for the boy scouts, smoking weed was burning dead grass, and listening to your transistor radio was listening to your tranny, though now the connection is obvious, and to go on a trip you would go out for a day on a Happy Times charabanc, nowadays we all have to be careful of the words we choose for the fear of upsetting anyone or even fear of prosecution, imagine going down the pub seeing your mates, 'where you been today Pete?' my reply would have to be, 'I have been out with my tranny, camped up with Flash and Danny Dare, we were all gay, we smoked some weed and went on a trip!' They would have kicked me out the bar and relegated me to the snug with a milk stout.

By 1954 we were starving hungry all the time so, we decided to dig an area of the bombsite we called the garden, it was heavy claggy soil because the Holders had raised their garden to avoid flooding in the winter, which in turn flooded ours so much it looked like a paddy field, we had found books on gardening and growing crops on the tip and we could buy cheap seeds from the ironmongers across the road, if the Holders could do it so could we, we slaved away most of the summer, carting the boulders and rubbish to the bottom of the garden, forming a moat against the water and building our den at the same time, after a few months of painstaking work turning over the heavy soil, with blisters as big as two-bob pieces, we managed to grow sprouts, cabbages and potatoes - which were often blighted with grubs from the Cabbage White Butterfly - we had grown a dinner table for every creature under the sun and spent most of our time fending off the creatures that came for a free feed, but there was still enough for us and once we had picked the grubs out and peeled the spuds and sprouts, we would cook them in a tin can in our den and eat them with gusto, there's something about home-grown produce that far surpasses farmed produce, so when Tommy saw how good we were he gave us the job permanent, he even managed to get five ton of horse manure delivered, how it did stink, we had to do all the work, shovelling and transporting it with the old pram we used to collect the coal and Val in, and then mulching the manure in the soil for days on end of back-breaking work, then, as with all things when Tommy got involved, it became a burden not a pleasure, every year we were made to grow food for all of us, by the time I was seven we had become self-sufficient and able to feed ourselves. We reinforced the Berlin Wall so the Holders could not sneak over and pinch our veg and woe betide any moles that came for a free feed. It was about this time that Tommy had one of his greatest brainstorms, this was to get us fruit picking, probably inspired by our efforts at self-sufficiency and also to line his pockets, from then on any school holidays, including Saturdays and Sundays we had spare, were banned, it was up in the morning at five o'clock to catch the covered lorry that the farm would send to pick us up at designated pickup points, packed in the back with other waifs and strays we would make the half hour journey to Bradshore's Farm near Cosford, that's probably where Tommy got the horse manure from, then to work eight to ten hours a day picking blackcurrants for a few shillings, the days dragged endlessly with the boredom, then wise Ron noticed the farm hands never emptied the baskets of fruit when we weighed them in, they would pay us the money for the baskets of fruit and just stack them for transport after weighing, so Ron told Tommy, hence Scrooge and the Artful Dodger concocted a plan, they would put a large flat stone in the bottom of the basket, you know like a piece of slate, to give it extra weight, then cover it with black currents, no one ever knew, even the farmer was unaware, the first time when we weighed in there were hardly any black currents covering the stone, we were panicking because they would often scoop the currents out by hand to get the designated weight and this would expose the fraud, so we later elaborated it and they never cottoned on. After that, we spent most of the time skiving and playing around the farm, lozocking in the sun, once we had done Tommy's quota of six baskets a day, Tommy was happy and so were we. It was around this time that I made my bond with my Mother Earth, there in those fields I could sit amongst the wheat, the corn and barley, hidden from the evils of this world, listening to the whispering of Mother's children as they danced amongst the breeze, and whilst that breeze was breathing would sit in the woods and the majestic trees would bow to me, and whilst watching the diamonds dancing on the lake the sun would comfort me and a calmness would descend within me, lying calmly there in the eye of the storm of this life, this was the place where food and love came from, the trees and the earth, and no food, no comfort, no compassion, no love, nothing ever came from the gates of Eden.

The following year the farmers had cottoned on, especially when we got it down to one berry in the basket lying on a pile of stones, such is greed, and they then used a different method to weigh the fruits. The juices of the fruits would stick to your hands making them tacky and after a while the smell of them used to make me feel sick and still does even to this day, however it did once pay for a well-deserved holiday for all of us which was very rare in those days, it was the only one we ever had, Elsie forced Tommy to take us, he had piles of money to waste earned by us but not spent on us, on that only holiday we were all crammed in a little caravan on a site, for food Tommy fished for crabs on the pier and we collected winkles on the beach, in the evening he would boil them in a pot alive, it used to make my flesh creep the strange sound of the crabs writhing in agony, screeching the side of the huge pot with their claws trying to get out, never could get the courage up to eat the slops and to this day can't stand the thought of eating shellfish. There was a large swimming pool on the site with loads of people in and around it, walking near the edge something or someone pushed me and, plummeting into the water and not being able to swim, the pool sloped from three-feet to sixteen-feet deep, the more panic the further down the slippery slope to the bottom under water my floundering body

Pete Davies

went, this went on for what seemed eternity, instinctively pushing myself off the bottom towards the light, gasping for air, breaking the surface only to sink back even deeper, the distance from the bottom to the top was getting longer and longer, my lungs where filling with water, splashing about for what seemed two to three minutes, gulping the chlorinated water into my lungs, my mind was drifting, then suddenly, as though awoken from a dream, found myself lying prostrate on the poolside chlorinated water gurgling out of every orifice of my body, sitting up my throat was burning, my lungs stinging, coughing and choking up water, there were people around me, not looking at me, just sitting about acting normal, going about their business, you would have thought that if someone had rescued me, stopped me drowning, there would be some sort of commotion over my demise and the hero who had rescued me would be standing over me, telling everyone how wonderful he was, but no, someone had pulled me out when semi-conscious and must have lain me there, but whoever it was saved my life that day, the sun was blazing down and my lungs were sore and no one even looked at me. After a short while bewildered and shuddering, my search for the rest of the family commenced, to eventually find them sitting on deckchairs about ten yards away beside the pool in a corner oblivious to everything, I never said anything to a soul of my trauma but have always wondered who got me out and why there was no commotion and from that day I have always kept well clear of deep water, my guardian angel, who checks on me from time to time, looked after me again on that day and it's pretty obvious to me when reading these writings that he keeps saving me for some reason.

With the summer gone and the ground turning cold there came the dreaded winter, freezing and bleak, there was no fruit picking and getting up at five, but then there was the other side of the coin: on Saturdays the coal had to be collected. There was something magical about the early morning street scenes, the way the virgin snow lay on the ground two-feet deep, turning the otherwise drab black-and-white scenery into a wonderland of glistening silver white. The Coal Warf was just across the main road which was deadly to cross being so busy, and when the thick fog came down, caused by coal fires and the industrial surround, it was treacherous, on one occasion when attempting to cross the foggy main road, it was early evening and the night had set in about five o'clock, this was the busy time, everyone finished work at five in those days and there would be a surge of traffic and people. With Mike, my cousin, in tow we had to cross the road to get to the sweet shop, we stepped off the curb onto the main road and into the mist and fog to the sound of frustrated bus drivers crawling along cursing to theirselves about the conditions, some walking in front of their lorries or vans with flashlight's beam not even cutting one foot through the soupy mixture, you could see the hazy lights of the shops opposite, not clear, just giving an eerie glow as though calling you, like a siren calling a captain of an old galleon onto the deadly rocks, enticing you to dare, offering great rewards like a gob stopper or a packet of swizzles should the brave soul reach the other side, the lights urging you on like a welcoming beacon, luring you on, not holding Mike's hand tight enough, losing my grip he was gone, 'Mike, Mike, where are you?' He had gone in the mist, the dark dank mist, then the fear, the terror, the calamity, the shouting, at that moment one lone voice from the dense mist, 'he's under the car,' came a voice from the crowd of faceless beings shuffling along, 'get an ambulance,' the voice said, the commotion attracted the occupants of the houses we lived in including Joyce, Mike's mom, who was visiting us at the time, she never panicked, was calm and did everything by the book, she spread the crowd, nursed and held Mike in her arms whilst she sat on the road, with Mike in her arms, till the ambulance came, which took quite a while due to the conditions, her training kicking into gear, she was a nurse in the forces and a professional, Mike only suffered cuts and bruises because the cars were only crawling along in the thick fog and Joyce never held me responsible over the incident and never punished me for stupidity, being grateful to her for that, the guilt in my mind far outweighed any punishment that could be meted out, the road was always bustling with all sorts of traffic, horses and carts and delivery vans and, on Saturdays, tanks would rumble past, churning up the road on their way back to the barracks, coming back from manoeuvres on Cannock Chase. That road was also the test run for the Guy Bus Factory which was a couple of miles down the road, where they once made all sorts of army trucks and tanks for the war effort, the test drivers would sit on the open chassis with nothing to protect them from the freezing conditions and the elements, looking like snowmen when the blizzard winds blew.

During the long winter's wait, often watching from the window, to the left of our house was a bus stop where some of the workers would gather in the snowflake storm, the queue often twenty or thirty people deep, beneath them a black patch of ground where the snow had been melted by the warmth of their feet stamping to increase the circulation of blood, and bodies shuffling, trying to keep warm whilst waiting for the bus to arrive and transport them to their factory for the day, hovering above the queue, mixed with the cold air, a plume of blue and white smoke from the first Woodbine or Park Drive of the day. The trolley buses were the type that used to run on overhead electric cables, when the snow was heavy on the lines, the connecting poles would disengage in a spectacular display of sparks and the driver had to get out and reposition them with a large bamboo pole which he carried under the bus, hooking them back on to the cable to enable him to continue his journey, sometimes there would be a wonderful display of icicles stalagtiting down from the cables after a frosty night and, when the sun warmed up the air, they would come crashing down at random, had someone been directly below they could have been skewered by the huge spikes of ice, which would dissolve due to the warmth of the dead body thus producing no weapon of death, what a wonderful murder mystery for Sherlock Holmes or Agatha Christie to solve that would have been, *The Mystery of the Ice Dagger* they could call it, anyway this busy road was a challenge for a seven-year-old lad and an old frame of a perambulator with rickety wheels made it even more of a challenge, the pram would wobble on its wheels and transporting a hundredweight bag of coal was an added strain, once I reached the gates of the Coal Warf, there was a queue of elderly and young that had formed there also waiting to be served, some, like me, were hardly dressed for winter with their clothes in rags, the queues were long and it took about an hour standing in the snowflake showers and the deep snow freezing your legs and feet very rapidly, with holes in my shoes and wearing short trousers, it was hard to keep warm. The Warf was full of huge lumps of black wet shining coal and in the centre of the coal arena stood Daniels the coalman, about five-feet-four in height, his stocky build necessary for hauling the one hundredweight bags off his cart and on his back down entries and alleyways, his jet black horse, Satan he called him, was well looked after, tethered in a stable in the corner of the yard, for without Satan the blackness that burned like the fires of hell could not be delivered. Daniels wore a flat cap that shone at the peak, his baggy pants were held up by a thick belt and braces, these shone with black coal dust and sweat as did his jacket and waist coat, the whites of his eyes and the redness of his lips were the only clean part of his person and were exaggerated by the blackness of his face, he stood like a gladiator in his coliseum of coal surrounded by an open arena where he plied his trade, sledge hammer in one hand, coal bag in the other, looking like a trident and net to a young imaginative lad, glaring at me, 'next,' he would shout, stepping into his world and arena, dragging a large black hessian bag from the pile that lay in the sludge, painting the back of my legs and short trousers with thick black coal residue, the bags were heavy even when dry, when it rained it was a double-edged sword for Daniels, the slack, the coal and the bags weighed heavier resulting in more profit, on the other hand it gave him a wash which irritated him. Dragging the bag towards the scales with both hands Daniels would grab it off me with great ease and throw it on the scales, down would come his sledgehammer smashing a huge lump of coal into smithereens splinters of coal and slack ricocheting everywhere, when Daniels started to fill the hemp bag piping up, 'no slack please Mr Daniels,' he would stop and glare at me, piercing me with the whites of his eyes for a second or two, he knew that, even at that age, I was wise to him, being an expert on coal, having collected so much, so he could not slip any batts in the bag. The slack was just a powder residue of the coal which weighed heavier when soaking wet and the batts were pieces of slate which looked like coal to the untrained eye and would explode with a tremendous force once put on an open coal fire, often blowing the contents of the grate clear across the room to result in burning embers flying everywhere, Tommy had learned me well, suffering the belt on occasions of lapse, Daniels would lift the hundredweight bag full of coal onto the old pram, it would creak and groan under the weight, whilst dragging it and pushing it across the main road to get it back to the house, after that I would take the coal out of the bag and stack it in the coal house, a small dry room to the side, and once that was done, Tommy would appear with the key twirling round his grubby gloved finger and lock the coal-house door so the coal could only be used at his command because coal was a valuable commodity and expensive. The next job was to return back across the road with the coal bag on the pram and give it back to Daniels who would fling the bag on to the pile to await the next customer, then back across the road once more to park the rickety dirty old pram in the air-raid shelter to await the next coal delivery or even the next babbie.

Tommy and Elsie never went out much but when they did they would go to the dog races on a Friday night mostly funded by the fruits of our labour, they would go to a place called Monmore Green Dog Track, there was no one to care for Dianne, Ron or me, so we had to wing it down the bottom of the garden till they came back, they would leave about six in the evening and return about twelve-thirty midnight. It was pitch black after ten o'clock and, when the evening shadows fell the cold would chill our bones, on the winters nights the mist would hover two feet above the Somme sometimes lit by the silvery moon so we would huddle together in our den at the bottom of the garden and often light a fire, and we could not get in the house, they locked the door, it was all confusing to me being the age of five, Ron was six and a half, Dianne about eight, one particular evening two strangers came to the house when Tommy and Elsie were not there, curiously walking up the garden negotiating the weeds and nettles to see who it was, a man ran towards me picked me up, held me high in the air above his head and called me his son, he happily toyed with me and the floating sensation made me laugh, the tears of joy that ran down my face were soon to be turned into waves of sorrow, he stayed a short while till his female companion who, irritated by his actions, dragged him away, he put me down on the ground, walked away from me and, looking back pensively, there was a glint of tear to his eye, standing there in my own pools of tears, alone, feeling bare and naked to his world, 'please don't walk away from me,' I wished, 'spare one thought for me', I wished, 'take me with you,' I wished. I wished in vain. They both melted back into the devastated foggy ruins of my mind and from that night were never to be seen again, even to this day it amazes me that anyone could do that, see three kids alone in the dark and turn their backs, walk away and do nothing. Who is the worse? Tommy who knew the secret, who kept and fed me, knowing full there was a cuckoo in the nest? Or my birth father, the one who was responsible but was prepared to dump this responsibility on others? These are the things that burn in my mind, the complete disregard of responsibility which you can see even to this day in the lives of many, and it's one of the reasons I don't know who I am, where I am or what I am.

It was 1954 and it was about that time that Arthur, Geoff, Barry and Joyce came on the scene, Arthur was on leave from the army, Joyce on leave from the W.R.E.N.S. Jeff from touring and Barry on leave from Borstal approved school, these were the kids from Elsie's first and only marriage, they were my half-brothers and the rest of us were just bastards by birth in the eyes of the law. All the Alcott's were stocky lads in their stature, they far outweighed the Davises although Geoff was lighter, maybe it was all the dancing he did that kept his weight down, Ron and I were between the two statures, in later years the difference between Ron and me was plain to see with me resembling the Alcott's and Dave taking on the features of Tommy, but Ron, well he was like neither of us, for instance Dave was thin with a full head of hair, Ron was stocky with bushy curly hair and me, the same build and no hair at all.

Arthur was born in the year 1930 in Mary Ann Street, Piper's Row, Hoarsely Fields, to Arthur William Alcott and Elsie, my mother, who then became Elsie May Alcott, they were married at Horsley Fields Chapel and Arthur's dad, Elsie's only husband, was a steel erector who travelled the country to do his work. At that time they lived in what was called a Hoth, which was a square of houses with one alley leading to the centre, at the age of seven Arthur was hailed a schoolboy hero, walking home one day he spotted a young girl, her name was Margaret Langford, her clothes were ablaze, he did what anyone else would do so he said, he put his coat over her and put out the fire, this action burnt his hands but that was nothing in those days because people were tough and just got on with it whatever it was, the local paper, the *Express and Star* hailed him a hero and he was presented a medal for bravery by the Mayor. Arthur joined the army cadets, probably also inspired by the stories of Elsie, and there he learned to be a boxer, this became a godsend to him. He wasn't called up for national service he volunteered, he boxed for his regiment the 15th/19th Hussars, the tank regiment part of the famous Desert Rats. Before he volunteered, he worked at the British Bath Foundry, probably conscripted by Tommy, making steel baths for eight shilling a bath, it was a dirty filthy job and hard graft and it took most of the day to make a bath, you know, the old cast-iron ones with the claw feet, they had to be perfect and if there were any flaws to the casting you were not paid for it so it was called piece work, to be in the army was a lot better than that so that's the reason he joined, from 1948 Arthur served ten years doing national service, with me being only one year of age at the beginning of his service. His first job was to drive a half-track and he was stationed in Germany. Elsie once told me that she went to the pictures with a friend about 1950 and, lo and behold, on *Pathe News* was a clip of Arthur with the Seventh Armoured Division, the half-track he drove was stuck in a ditch in Lübek, Germany, the steel caterpillar track had come off, he stood beside the halftrack hands on hips laughing his head off, he was a corporal at the time. Knowing Arthur he got some hapless private to drive the vehicle without a license and after that put him on charge, he often played such pranks for a laugh. One of the men started to hammer the track back on, Elsie says she saw Arthur flinch to one side, but thought nothing of it. A year or so passed and Arthur was making a name for himself as the unbeaten heavyweight champion for the regiment, once asking him how come he was never beaten, he said, to me, all my opponents just looked upon it as a free pass to go anywhere, which it was, but they never took it seriously which he did. He later went into the regimental police, in the police it was one of his tasks to do guard duty, on one occasion one of the prisoners said, if he did not get his bed changed regular he would hang himself, Arthur, being what he was, said, 'here,' and threw him a piece of rope, 'here hang yourself,' see if he cared. Next morning, there hanging from the bars, was the prisoner stone dead. Another time he went to inspect a cell and a prisoner had rubbed his shoes in his own excrement and made foot marks all over the walls and ceiling of the cell, when Arthur saw the mess he said 'what have you been doing,' 'walking in my sleep, Corporal Alcott,' was the reply. This prisoner, through his boredom, had a small copper mustard tin which he polished daily, it was circular at the open end and shone due to the continual polishing, noticing it on the table glinting in the sun that shone through the bars of his cell window, it caught Arthur's eye, he picked it up, held the prisoner down and banged three circles on his forehead with the tin, the force had drawn the blood and cut deep, 'don't do it again, get this place cleaned up and that's to remember me by,' said Arthur. The odd irony is that, twenty years later, long after Arthur had left the army walking down the street in his home town, he noticed a traffic warden about to place a ticket on his car, he went over to the car and, as warden turned round, on his forehead he had three circles, Arthur said, 'private stand to attention,' 'pardon sir we have never met,' the warden said. Just as he was about to stick the ticket on Arthur's car, Arthur chirped up, 'Lübek 1953,' the warden scarpered taking the ticket with him, you see you can never hide your past, it will catch up with you one day, it may take a long time to take the full circle but, believe me, it will return. These are some of the stories he told me, there must have been many more, and this was the torturer Ron and I had to suffer when he came home from leave, playing his tricks at every opportunity. In later years when he had mellowed with age, I asked Arthur why he had done these things, he said, being a corporal in the military police, had he not disciplined the prisoners so and let them get away with it, he would have been the one in those cells, not them, that's the way it was, and it was his job and he had absolute power, he said you never realize how power can be such a drug until you have had it. I replied, 'but surely, because you had that power over man to do as you saw fit, surely compassion and doing nothing is a greater power knowing full well you can?' He looked at me bewildered. He told me he once shot a man dead who was attacking one of the senior officers and court martial proceedings against him followed, when he was taken in front of the commanding officers, his reputation as boxer for the regiment and a desire to sign on for another four years' service quashed the case. He intended to go professional and would have probably done well but - remember the half-track incident when Elsie was at the pictures - unknown to him at the time a shim of metal had splintered off the half-track and lodged in the back of his eye, thus finishing his boxing career, and people tell me there is no such thing as karma, or was that just another case of the unwritten justice Elsie preached. In his later years, Jean managed to get him some compensation to help him in his retirement. At the age of eighty-two Arthur's mind has now gone, battered into oblivion by the endless boxing bouts of raging violence. Age and dementia are starting to take their toll, the once clever, cruel and active mind has now become sedated, the proud warrior is no more, and even a tear comes to my eye to see how the bewildered mind of my one-time persecutor has disintegrated into nothing, all those years on this earth for what? We sat in the ladies ward at the hospital only a few weeks ago Marlene, his German wife, had been taken ill due to age and circumstance, Arthur sat there, wondering where he was, looking around the ward, confused by all the sick women lying in the beds, some with legs exposed and slips showing due to the trauma of not being bothered and feeling ill, when humans are really ill dignity seems to take second place. He asked me, whilst scratching the top of his head with cap in hand and a puzzled look on his face, and, I suppose, with a flash memory from his distant past, 'are we in a brothel?'

Barry, my other half-brother, loved guns and violence, he took up boxing as well, he seemed to live the lifestyle of a cowboy, if he walked in any bar, street or club should any person give him just a look, it would usually end up in an affray of some sort or even pistols at dawn, his boxing and his violent attitude stood him in good stead in Borstal and all the other remand homes and prisons he often attended throughout his early years, this was where he spent most of his teenage life, where he was bound in life no one knew, he was a couple of years younger than Arthur and, in his later years, he became a bouncer in the pubs and clubs. Barry would often leave guns and bullets and various weapons lying around the house, one time Ron found a Luger pistol, the type the German army used in the war, whoever put it there no one knows, we found it on a high shelf in the scullery with some boxes of bullets, we were about six or seven years of age at the time, we took it down our bunker and Ron managed to work out how to put the bullets in, with me trying to make them bang by hitting them between large stones. Just as Ron was about to plug me in the head, Barry came down the garden took the gun off Ron and clouted us both. A few days later sitting in our bunker at the bottom of the garden Barry stood at the top of the garden about fifty yards away with his air rifle, it was a B.S.A. 22, he was targeting various items that he had set up, his favourite targets were pegs off the line, I stuck my head out of the trench and shouted to Barry, 'bet you can't hit me from there,' whilst thumbing my nose at him, he changed his aim and turned the rifle towards me, 'there's no way,' my mind thought, 'that he could hit me from that distance,' then watching the pellet on its trajectory, though in slow motion each frame click, click, clicking, at one second intervals, the pellet got nearer and nearer for one split second my brain said move now, a fraction too late the slug hit me straight between the eyes but on the bony part of my forehead, at the time I never gave any thought to it, but doesn't it seem strange that at that age I saw the pellet on its trajectory even at speed, slowed down by my mind, giving me just enough time to avoid a major injury like losing an eye? What a shot, holding my head and slumping back into the trench in agony, Barry came running up, 'don't tell Tommy or Elsie and we will take you out rabbit hunting,' after a short while the pain ceased and so did the tears and looming was a fabulous day out with the two killers, they kept their word - I kept mine, there was a choice of guns, a snub-nosed revolver suited me fine, twirling it round my trigger finger like Billy the Kid, they could have nicknamed me Baby-Faced Pete had I chosen the Bren gun they offered me, but it was too heavy for me to carry, when you pulled the trigger it was uncontrollable for a small lad like me, we stayed out all day for me to return an empty handed hunter with his gun. But we took Barry and Arthur's spoils, skinned them, gutted them, stuck them in a pot, boiled them and ate them, oh what times, sitting there chewing the rabbit meat and spitting the buck shot out and by the age of seven had learned to skin and gut a rabbit on my own, and from that day on I inherited the job of pulling the entrails and guts out of the chickens when Elsie used to purchase them from the market for Tommy, they always came complete, not like nowadays filled with chemicals and water, gutted and trussed ready for the oven, it was one of the jobs Tommy allotted me, you see he had not got the guts to do it himself, if you will excuse the pun. One winter's night, lying in my bed with Ron and Dave, snug under the army coat, a copper's knock came to the door, can't stand coppers since they took James Cagney my hero away to the chair in the film *Angels with Dirty Faces*, and also from the time when Ron and I got ourselves a job as paper boys, we had managed to concoct two old bikes together with stuff from the tip, basically boneshakers, when one morning at six o'clock Ron approached the paper shop on his bike, peddling onto the footpath a couple of yards from the shop with me behind him, out of the hedge jumped this copper, as Jimmy would say, 'the dirty rat,' and he arrested Ron, I'm talking about an eleven-year-old kid here, he had to go to crown court for trial, well, the same building. Not sure what the outcome of the trial was, but Ron got a severe beating from Tommy, his screams were horrendous and he became the second criminal in the family. Later, there were several coppers at the door, they raided the house and took Barry and his armoury away, Barry had threatened one of the local farmers with a shotgun, apparently he had been rabbiting on the property and the farmer had grabbed the brace of rabbits Barry was carrying, 'hand back the rabbits or the leads coming your way,' that's what Barry said to the farmer, holding the shotgun to his face, the farmer obviously went to the police, they came to the house, took Barry away and sent him to jail because that was not the first time he had been a naughty boy, asking Elsie the next day where they had taken him, 'sewing mail bags,' was her sharp reply, when Barry was later conscripted into the army he spent most of his time on what they called jankers, scrubbing the floors with a toothbrush and scraping the latrines with a razor blade and in the 'glass house' as Elsie called it, but we never received any veg, which at that age I thought might have been perks of the job. When eventually he left the army, well he was chucked out, they were fed up of him, they said, he was too violent, he was admitted to a sanatorium, spent a few years locked away from mankind, to be released eventually as a normal person, they gave him a certificate when he came out to prove he was sane, come to think of it he is the only sane person I know in the eyes of the law, don't know of anyone else who can produce a certificate to prove they are normal, do you? He spent the rest of his life looking over his shoulder for fear of retribution from persons or people he had beaten up over the years as a bouncer in the local clubs, he and Arthur had many battles with the local Hell's Angels of the time and often they were very bloody. He eventually died of a cancer. That's the one thing you all need to fight against in this life that dirty sneaky disease which keeps raising its head, creeps up on you and cuts you down in your prime. Unfortunately, the fighting Barry was good at was not the solution to this enemy of us all, but don't despair of this, cancer does not always win because nothing is inevitable when it comes to the human spirit and willpower, there's another story to tell of a battle against cancer, which will be an inspiration to all those who have been unfortunate enough to look in to the face of this cowardly killer.

Then there was Jeff, he was the youngest of the Alcotts, you could tell Jeff had not done national service, his character had not been bent or twisted out of shape by the pliers of authority, he was like my art teacher once described my art work - no, not 'crap' - he said to me, 'you can tell you are self-taught because you have no bad habits, no repetitiousness in the style'. This was Jeff, he was never miserable, always cheerful, he came and went so quickly he would visit the house then be gone for months on end, but when he was around he cheered me up with his ridiculous funny stories and jokes, 'read this really good book the other day, Pete,' he would say, getting me interested, 'it's called, *All About Stairs and Landings* by Roger Bannister,' or, 'saw a good film the other day, Anna Neagle and Joseph Cotton in *The Thread*.' Probably not funny to most people but to a child in my situation it brightened up my day. He was also a kind of showman, always making up his own lines to popular songs of the time and making them funny, and he was a brilliant dancer, I often listened in to the conversations between him and Elsie about the competitions he would enter, he could jitterbug, roller dance and rock and roll and jive, he was a professional and the ladies loved him, these were the dances of the Fifties that the G.I.s bought over from America in the Forties during occupation, before D-day. Jeff was always up and down the country dancing at various venues, like a British Gene Kelly, come to think of it he never had what some people called a proper job like a factory slave or a lesser person wasting his life on a nine-till-five job, Jeff had this freedom to choose with no responsibilities, he just did not care, he was happy and a free spirit. Look into some people's eyes and you can see the envy poisoning their mind against others who are truly free, people will say they are free but what they really envy is seeing true freedom in others, thinking full well that this can never happen to them; freedom grows in the mind and blooms like a flower. Anyone who had working class roots and never had a 'proper job' and wanted to better themselves to do something different was looked down upon by other working-class families as a wastrel, a 'never-do-well' they were called in those days and I was classed the same. Jeff had compassion for me and he had this flippant attitude, he never scolded me or punished me or hit me for anything, with Jeff I felt safe and comfortable, but maybe that's because I would behave myself and sit listening to my Scheherazade, fascinated by his stories and tales, he was definitely my mentor, often he would say to me, 'Pete here's half a crown, go down Sammy's and get me a Bounty Bar and a bottle of Dandelion and Burdock pop,' upon my return he would share it with me, give me half the Bounty and a good swig of the pop, it was wonderful. It's strange how one kind act can stay in your mind for all time and the memories remain, I still have fond memories of Jeff and have modelled some of myself on his carefree attitude to life, snubbing my nose at authority and laughing at serious people and how they make everything so depressing, it's possible for me to turn a miserable situation into something positive, my glass is always full in anticipation for all things, to me Jeff was like a mischievous magical little imp, here today gone tomorrow, then he stopped coming to the house, he did not die or anything, just never came, never saw him again even to this day, but still have my memories and a brotherly love for the passing dancing clown named Jeff.

Now the last of nine kids born to Elsie, was Joyce, the first time ever I saw her she came home on leave from the W.R.E.N.S., Ron had been messing about with one of her records trying to play it, she had an old gramophone in the hall, the type you wound up and the needles were like panel pins which fitted into the playing arm, and I sometimes used them to nail my sole or heel back on my shoe but they only worked for a short while till the thing would start flapping again. Joyce walked into the house and there was Ron, he had scratched one of her records and was now confronted by her shouting and bawling at him, the outcome was she smashed the record over Ron's head to send him off in tears and pain. I searched him out to find him crying in the air-raid shelter, sat by him, and put my arm around him and said 'bet it was *don't be Cruel* by Elvis,' 'why do you think that?' he said, sobbing, 'because it was a smash hit,' I said giggling. Joyce was always smart in her military uniform, after she left the W.R.E.N.S she married this war hero, his name was Dennis Kennedy, his warship the *H.M.S. Wizard* was a W-class destroyer deployed in north Norway to protect the aircraft carrier *Searcher*, against air attack, also he was deployed at Scapa Flow providing cover on D-day to prevent interference from German battleships during the beach assaults and allied landings, later he was deployed off the coast of Japan to aid the repatriation of Japanese servicemen held at Hamamatsu, and later still the ship was converted to a sub hunter, so you can see he deserved his medals. They used to live in Wombourn, just outside Wolverhampton, they had one lad, Mike, and three daughters, Mike was a few years younger than me, he was the one who got run over in the fog that fateful night, Ruth was the eldest daughter and Rita and Roberta were twins. Elsie used to visit Joyce and sometimes took me with her, after a while I visited on my own, travelling by bus, there were wide fields to play in and there was a lot of countryside and the house was clean which was part of the fascination, till one day for some reason, Dennis put his hand up my short trousers and felt my behind, don't ask me why but somehow from instinct I knew that this was wrong, maybe that's just me and my common sense, from then on I never went to visit there again and never told anyone. You may think, why not tell anyone? The reason is that for a young person to stand and accuse an adult of something was unheard of in those days, he was a World-War-Two navy hero who was covered in medals for bravery, no one would have listened to me and it probably would have ended up with a clout for lying and caused me more trouble. Sometime later they immigrated to Australia on one of those ten-pound trips organized in the late Fifties, it took the boat about six months to get there according to the correspondence sent to Elsie from Joyce. Apparently she met a bloke on the boat, dumped Dennis after finding out he was gay and lived with this new man in Australia. She put the kids in Barnardo's homes, very cold-hearted of her, last time there was any news of them was the late Sixties. Elsie said Mike had joined the Aussie navy but what happened to the others, the twins and Ruth, was a mystery to me until the end of this book when I found out about the demise of the others.

Pete Davies

Anyway now you have met the family, but there is one more curse to add and that is the one from Goering, the German Luftwaffe Air Marshal. Elsie called it the day 'the Luftwaffe landed' and 'Goering's revenge for not finding the factories to bomb in the war', this was the day Arthur bought his German wife to live with us, Marlene Spiel-Mann was her name, at least that was the name engraved on her brown leather suitcase when she parachuted in, they had come to lodge in the back room of our house, boy did she get a shock, if Hitler had seen it he would have called off the war and surrendered, thinking, 'what the hell do I want to invade this place for? It's worse than my bunker'. It was in a worse state than Dresden or Berlin after the Yanks, Brits and the Russians had laid siege. The Germans are a spotlessly clean and proud race so after the initial shock she set about cleaning the kitchen, the cooker was covered in grease and the kitchen had never seen soap or water ever, a flame thrower, a stick-grenade or even a bottle of *blitzkrieg* bleach would have been a good start, Marlene rolled her sleeves up and started to scrub, she cleaned and scrubbed the walls, ceilings and floors till the foul stench and all the grease had gone, this narked Elsie and she took it as a personal snipe that she was lazy and dirty, which she was, so Elsie took every opportunity to bad mouth Marlene, often calling her a Nazi due to the fact that Marlene's father was a member of the Nazi Party during the war, Ron and I would take the mick, she would say to Arthur, at meal times things like, 'Artur, vud jou like some fish ent ships?' and we would elaborate on this, making up our own sentences in broken German, we had learned this from the stories in the comics where we read about prisoners and 'ze var' and the dialect was similar to Marlene's, so we had plenty of material to choose from. We once read a story from the First World War on Christmas Day; allegedly the Germans and the Brits played each other at football. Ron came home once with a leather World-War-Two fighter pilot's helmet, he found it in the garden of some derelict cottages over the road, Ron would stand outside her door with me in tow the helmet plonked on my head, scruffy, dirty faced and needing to blow my nose, when Marlene appeared at the door Ron would give her a Nazi salute and say things like 'isle ikla' 'today, zis young British airmen vill play football, to varm us up he vill practice in ze minefields', goading her, Marlene would say to Arthur, 'Arta, zey are picking on me', and he would retaliate by clouting us and sometimes torturing us to get his own back, one of his favourite tricks was to tie us up back to back, trussed up like chickens with the rope tight around our necks and feet and hands bound behind our backs, and if you moved the rope would tighten around your neck and choke you so you had to keep still to breath, he would leave us for a couple of hours bound and gagged at the bottom of the garden in a trench, no doubt one of his army tricks from his head-torturing days as a prison guard. Hitler once reputedly said he would wring the English neck like a chicken's, and Churchill replied, 'some chicken, some neck', and maybe Arthur, influenced by Marlene, was just practicing by 'obeying ze orders', in later years Marlene told me she was sixteen when the war broke out and she was drafted into the German air force, I was going to say 'machine gunning ze Tommy' but that would be just wishful thinking, her job was pushing marker pegs across boards in an underground bunker for the Führer, but by the way she cleaned our house I would say her more likely employment was polishing the doodle bugs before they were launched towards London. When she and Arthur came to England she left a son behind with relatives in Germany, she told me of the carnage when the Russians came raping and pillaging and of her pre-existence living in a cellar in bombed out Berlin, had it not been for Arthur befriending her family and her son - he gave the family food which he had confiscated from black market criminals and such - the path she would have taken in life would be so much different, she told me of her brother of eighteen who died on the last day of the war and was posthumously awarded the Iron Cross second class given to brave German soldiers for close combat duties, which she has to this day and is proud of, every Christmas when she hears the tune *Silent Night* you could see a tear in her eye, this stems from times of war and the loved ones she lost because no one wins at war as time has proven. In comparison, Elsie once told me of her elder brother Albert, he was a showman always doing card tricks, juggling and entertaining the kids in the street, when he was called up in 1914 to fight for England he fought in the trenches in France, he often cheered up the doomed soldiers with his comical antics and tricks, for four years he fought and he survived the carnage, blood and terror, dodging bullets and death, 'kamerad', 'kamerad', the surrendering German soldier shouted hands high in the air as Albert buried the cold steel bayonet deep in his chest, one of the gruesome stories of the battles he told his mother and that Elsie narrated to me as a young lad, it could almost have been Marlene's brother had it been the other war. When Albert arrived home from that lousy war he sat on the garden wall, the kids came round, he was still in his army gear, 'show us a trick,' they would say, 'show us a trick Albert'. One of his tricks was to put a coin in his mouth and make it disappear, the kids would force his mouth open, look inside amazed at finding nothing there, then Albert would pretend to choke and, lo and behold, the coin would pop out on the end of his tongue, but not that day, he swallowed it and it choked him to death, so in the end both were killed by cold steel in one form or another, what irony, Those two stories are typical of the brave kids and men who fight these wars. Though a stoic and a Brit there is compassion in my heart for all victims of war, friend or foe, except for the ones who hide beneath a religion or a hood, walking round with their fists clenched in anger, shooting-in-the-back, trying to kill and maim, inflicting maximum pain, the cowardly faceless ones that have their own small vendettas against the world and its nations in the name of some personal cause or gain. There's got to be a poem in there somewhere, maybe some poetic justice even.

The trouble with being a seventh-born is that we look at everything from a different perspective, the human race think that they are all powerful, they can kill, create wars, destroy, plan, decide, choose, they discuss how they are destroying the planet, they think they are some kind of unique being, it is them being destroyed by their own ignorance and greed, Mother Earth is a gift given to you all to use as you please, to sit and feel the warmth of the sun, to watch it rise and set in all its splendour, to feel the calming influence of her great oceans, the freedom to walk her great mountain ranges, to breath the cool air, this should be enough, they say they are destroying the earth, how naïve they are, it is Mother Earth who will destroy them. Yes, they influence change with technology but the final decision will be made by Mother Earth. To think that they are capable of destroying her! When there is nothing left to destroy, what will be left is Mother. They give so-called prophesies of doom and gloom of the end of the world prophesised by Nostradamus and the Mayan calendar or any cranks trying to make a few bob, to my mind they will destroy your race with greed and corruption and change the function of Mother's nature, but, when they wipe theirselves out, our mother will still be here, awaiting the next smart-arses, she gives them all materials to build, food to eat, a cure for every ill, all they have to do is work it out, it's all here, a stepping stone to play with that shines at night and paves the way and another nine toys to reach the stars once the first step for mankind has been taken, after those planets there is infinity. There is everything you could possibly need, our mother knows that one day she will not be here, these are her gifts, her legacy to you her children if you want it, and these are things that can be touched, they are the reality and not hollow promises, what if, along the way, something has been missed, something important? After discovering electricity, harnessing energy, solving problems, progressing with medicine, what if there is something undiscovered which is of vast importance, is it the power to see beyond, into another dimension, an inner strength born to each of you? Some people may call it the Holy Spirit; it does not matter where the power comes from or what it is called, to me gods, crystals and images are focal points that can be used to open each of the many doors in your minds, are you misinterpreting everything? I once read these words in your bible 'In my father's house there are many mansions,' well! in your mind there are many doors, and each door capable of springing open in times of stress. To find the key and learn to control it is that the eternal answer? And are those doors the gateways to all things, which to a normal lifestyle (in other words, a closed mind) are classed as strange and mystical, and when individual doors are opened is it possible to witness paranormal events, to create powers of healing, receive flashes from your long forgotten past, even visions of the future, like aliens and U.F.O.S (maybe looking in on yourselves) are these the things to come destined to be mankind's future opening your minds to eternal peace? At this stage of your evolution you seem to be doing nothing to advance yourselves peacefully and if you can survive this present carnage and suppress your animal instincts then you may have a future. Mother Earth knows that eventually she will be swallowed up by the life-giving Sun, the same Sun that gives will take away and eventually expand into a fiery red giant to incinerate all into nothingness, that same sun may become a white dwarf or a black hole dragging what's left into the muddy pool of darkness that you all fear, the darkness of the unknown. The inhabitants of this planet talk of being alone in the universe, if you were a terrestrial visitor would you show yourself, knowing what they do and how they live? No, neither will anything else with a thinking brain, the warlike race of this planet are not ready to receive or even tap into intelligence above their own station at this stage of their evolution, they would use the power to kill, and destroy, it's in their nature, just like they are destroying and killing theirselves now. People are brainwashed from an early age to choose a path and they don't have many choices. Don't believe you go to hell, believe and go to heaven, well, the fantasy heaven they have created is already here and so is the hell, it's up to you the compassionate people of this world to unite against the humanoid despots who run this planet, who thrive on war and death, as soon as they learn to live in peace, or disappear from the face of this earth maybe just maybe the remainder of us will be allowed the key to open our minds which could be the doorway to the 'Promised Land'.

The years passed, Ron, Dianne and I were at junior school and Tommy had found a new hobby – meddling. He bought a television for his own use and locked it away, no one else was allowed to use it, it was one of those in a cabinet with doors on and a tiny dull screen, he was never satisfied with the reception, we would watch him through the window trying to get reception by standing in all sorts of positions with the dartboard-type aerial in his hand. he would be standing on a chair, no good, hold it high above his head, no good, on the floor, tut-tut-tutting away with the telly hissing and no picture, he would take the back off and start meddling about inside with a knife and fork, twisting knobs and prodding valves and generally poking about with the power surging through it, he could not read very well, on the back were the explicit instructions 'no meddling' and a picture of a lightning bolt which he completely ignored, there was always a danger he would get a massive shock, no such luck, he did get a couple of small ones but that only made him meddle a bit faster. When he got bored with messing with the television he bought himself a motorbike and sidecar and all the kit, a stupid helmet, gauntlet gloves, dressed like Rommel in full-length leather coat, he might have got it off Marlene, maybe that Luger was hers as well, the first day he sat on the motorcycle he had never ridden on one before, he kick-started it, sat on the saddle, stuck it into gear, let the clutch out, shot across the main road and hit a lamp post, to spend three days in hospital, what bliss and peace we all had.

There was a similar incident with Jeff. Arthur and Barry were now a terrible twosome, Arthur on leave from the army, Barry out of prison, they joined forces for torturing at every opportunity, Jeff was sitting on Arthur's motorcycle, a Triumph Bonneville, a powerful bike of the time, and Jeff had never ridden on a bike before and asked Arthur for a lesson. It was parked half way down the garden, 'how does this work,' said Jeff, 'kick start it like this,' Arthur said, 'click that into gear and when you let that lever out turn that handle quick'. Well!, Jeff shot up the garden straight through the French windows of the back of the house, the bike, the French windows and Jeff were demolished, all Arthur and Barry did was laugh their heads off, that was the mentality of them both. With me thinking, you have just destroyed an expensive motorcycle for a laugh, why? There again they may have stolen it, I ran down the garden for cover knowing there was going to be a confrontation between Elsie and them, but there was never any sign of Tommy, he always kept away, Barry and Arthur where big in stature, not only did Tommy keep away from them, he kept away from Ron and me as well when they were around, so that was some sort of positive.

Ron and I would play for hours on the Somme recreating famous battles often challenging each other to see who was the best soldier, me with my red cross of Saint George on a white background, my precious and a hand-crafted shield made from the bottom of an oak water-barrel, Ron with a homemade Roman spear, his flag a white cross on a white background, and Ron had the same sporting skills as an Italian general being a bloody good runner, I eventually cornered him, only for him to surrender once again. Through the corner of my eye at the top of the garden about sixty yards away a lone bowman stood with a long bow, that bow was twice as tall as me and was a part of Arthur and Barry's armoury, and that bow would succumb to one master only, knowing of it well and often having tried to draw it to no avail, only a trained archer or a strong person could draw it and that person was Arthur, lowering my shield and watching him raise the bow to the sky, then watching the trajectory of the arrow in awe and fascination as it sped and disappeared into the blue, for my eye was keen and if that arrow was slick I knew it could pierce through armour no matter how thick, as it arced through the blue sky a dot appeared right above me, raising my shield above my head instinctively, the arrow bounced off at an angle, judging by the trajectory it would have pierced my neck and passed down towards my heart had it not glanced the shield, don't ask me how my instinct worked but it did, how was that possible to do that at the age of seven? Maybe the fear of my message from Elsie was stirring up strange dark forces and they were trying to shoot the messenger.

Arthur, bought two pairs of small boxing gloves back with him from Germany, they fitted Ron and me perfectly, unknown to us at the time this was just another form of entertainment for Arthur and Barry, they would entice the two of us to box each other for a purse of half a crown to the winner providing the winner knocked out the opponent, the prize of half a crown was well worth fighting for, some people may think that it is hardly likely that two young kids could have the power and strength to knock each other out, this was Arthur's aim not ours, there was two occasions when, at a very early age, I was knocked out, once by a half house-brick that Ron threw at me from the top of the air-raid shelter, it hit me on the back of the head knocking me out, for me to attend Doctor Ghasper's to have the gash sewn up, and the second time when at school, being the wicket keeper, one of the snoots took a swing at the cricket ball missed and hit my head instead, for me to lose consciousness for a couple of minutes - so surely boxing gloves could do the same? And maybe, it was those two events that opened my brain to kick-start the strange events I am writing about today. The two human gods we represented stood over us refereeing with a wet towel, should we slack or appear to be spineless, the snaking wet towel would bite a part of bare flesh with the venom of a cobra adding a stinging pain to any part of our torsos, usually our bare spindly legs, Ron was bigger than me and, seeing through the blood, there were tears in his eyes as he rained blows, if only just to avoid the flicking venomous bite, which only fuelled the excitement for the onlookers, but those tears were for me, his younger brother, you see we loved each other, 'hit me, hit me back,' he would whisper, 'make a show, make a show', but my slender arms could not support the weight of the gloves for long and with my tiny form weakened from the heavy blows and the biting cobra and I often hoped my end would come soon, just like Jimmy's, on many occasions we were left with bloody noses and no money, after a while we wised up to their tricks and feigned unconsciousness to claim the purse, and, to their delight, they paid up not knowing we were throwing the fight, we had a pact that the first to bleed was the one to fall, we made a pretty sum out of them and would split the cash, those were the sort of games they would get up to when Arthur was on leave, but we had the measure of them both. On the day Arthur was due back to the barracks from leave, we pinched his army coat out of his kit bag, we used it on the flock, lumpy bed to keep us warm throughout the cold winters, in later years, talking to Arthur when he was a pensioner, he told me how he once lost his army coat and when he got back to the barracks he had to spend two weeks on duty on some remote moor freezing cold. I'm glad it was me who stole it - and it served him right.

5th November 1955, that was the day Arthur and Marlene left the lodgings in the back room of our house, they had managed to get one of those prefabricated bungalows, the ones that were built in the war years for short term and are still being lived in to this day, she also sent for her ten-year-old son from her previous marriage who was living in

Germany with her mother, his name was Hans, which was an appropriate name for in later years he turned out to be a thief and a bully just like the rest of the Alcotts, he was coming to England to live with them when they moved in. I remember that day well, being eight years of age at the time, it was one of the happiest days of my life at that point to see the back of them, Arthur got on his motorbike and Marlene got into the sidecar, with me watching them from the bottom of the garden. Arthur noticed me, got off his bike and came down the garden. I thought he was going to say goodbye to me but he came up and hit me on top of the head with a broom handle that had been propped up by the air-raid shelter where Elsie often parked her besoms after a night out, 'that's to remember me by,' he said, when he hit me there was a severe buzzing to my head and there were that many stars, which is what probably contributed to my near nervous-breakdown in later years and the strange events to come, I showed no pain so as not to give him any satisfaction, as far as I was concerned it was *auf wiedersehen*, good bye and good riddance and no more torture. And according to the stories in my comics I was so grateful that Arthur never married a Jap.

After November came Christmas, bah! Christmas, it's the falseness that gets me, good will to all men! with advertisements and billboards portraying the rich playing happy families in a fantasy world, sitting around a table stocked with food, in reality dreading the annual confrontation, no families ever visited us, no relatives, no cousins, no one, it was as though Tommy and Elsie were outcasts, for us it was always bleak and the workload increased, shovelling snow, getting the coal and that sort of thing, feet and clothes damp and freezing cold, but Tommy was in his element because this was miser season, anything he could steal he would, and with the Christmas spirit of Satan in him, he would go about his plans, every Christmas he would contribute to the decorations by stealing tins of industrial paint from where he worked to paint all the doors in the house, this obviously was a task for Ron and me, we would set about painting over the greasy doors, the paint was a horrible turquoise-blue colour with a smell like extra-strong pear drops that would take your breath away, we would put on a World-War-II gas mask each and worked away merrily like little elves, it was the paint they used to paint the machinery with at the factory during the shutdown in the main holidays, the problem was it never dried, it probably needed some sort of catalyst to add as a setting agent, after several weeks the doors become furry with the passing of jumpers, coats and such and by the end of the week we all looked like Smurfs, with the odd pot of gruel slopped down them the house would have looked very trendy - if you were a trapper or a mountain man. There again, Tommy could have scrounged some paint off Dennis and we would have had a living room painted the same grey colour as the W Class destroyer *H.M.S Wizard* and wandered around looking like Marley's ghost. When one of the food-dispensing machines had broken down at the works Tommy came home with loads of delicious-looking iced buns and sandwiches, we jumped on them and started to scoff as fast as we could when the taste hit our tonsils and the smell hit our nostrils, it was vile, they tasted of vulcanised rubber, they had been exposed to the smoking rubber fumes for hours, nothing he ever did was a success and nothing he ever stole was useful, about August every year he would obtain a goose or turkey chick from the rag-and-bone man, 'rags and bones, rags and tatters,' the rag-and-bone man would shout as he passed with his horse and cart, from a distance it sounded like 'eggs and owns', the silence shattered by the screaming banshee he called his trumpet, he would pass the houses his knackered old carthorse in front of the laden cart filled with rags and odd bits of tat, lead, copper and such, you could give him some old clothing or a bit of scrap metal and in return you could get a small chick, or even a bit of cash, maybe a penny depending on the value of your goods, we would look after the little chick, befriend it, feed it play with it, till Christmas Eve when Tommy would use endless methods to kill it, slamming its head in the door, stabbing its neck with a fork, eventually to slit its throat with a knife, sometimes causing the poor animal to run around the Somme bleeding and screaming with is throat half cut, when it did eventually die it was my job to find it and drag its carcass back to the house, pluck it and pull out its innards ready for Elsie to burn in the oven, then she would prepare the greens. 'Hubble, bubble toil and trouble, frogs and snails and puppy dogs' tails' passed through my mind at the time, the potted-meat factory down the road smelled better and that was where they used to slaughter the horses to turn them into glue, and that's probably where Elsie learned to cook, and needless to say I never had the stomach to eat poor little Billy. Tommy would buy himself a bottle of scotch whiskey some sherry and a bottle of port, once he opened them he would mark the line of fluid on the bottle with a pencil, he had not the brains to use a pen, and even if he had we had a backup plan to just top the bottle up with water, we would often take a swig and rub the mark out and put a new one back to the level of the drink, it tasted horrible as it went down burning our chests, we did this every year, it was a sort of ritual act of defiance against Tommy. Our Christmas presents consisted of an apple and an orange and some broken biscuits from the then-indoor market at Wolverhampton, remember the biscuits with the cow on them? we would spend hours trying to match the tail and the head, how exciting. One year we made Tommy a two-piece jigsaw as a gift but he couldn't do it, and we found an iron cooking pot buried down the garden so we cleaned it and gave it to Elsie for a present, but she burned a hole in it making rabbit glue, after Christmas came boxing day and all the sport and horse racing, this was when I got my season's beatings and my ears boxed, you could call it my Christmas box from the scruffs, Tommy's bets had to be taken over no man's land and the scruffs had new knuckledusters off Santa to beat you with, but once Christmas was over it was a relief and good riddance, then just the New Year to make a New Year's resolution which should be 'sod-the-coal ritual' and 'don't make any New Year's resolutions'.

By 1956, Ron, Dianne and I were well into junior school. Ron was more of an all-rounder than me so was Dianne, there were often small fights between kids at school and Ron at the age of ten had gained a reputation as someone who stood up for himself when picked on, and he often was, just because he was short sighted and wore National Health glasses, the kids would try to make fun of him and because his glasses were often mended with tape, you know the kind of jibes, calling him 'four eyes' and such, the same way they would pick on any kid who was slightly different, so you can see why Dave had no chance, he was too feeble to retaliate, but the retort from Ron would be much wittier than the other person's resulting in conflict which often ended in Ron pasting the perpetrators even though some of them where a lot bigger and older than him, this escalated and Ron gained a reputation as a tough little bugger which, with the boxing training and our lifestyle, yes we were, we were tempered like steel, at the age of ten we had to be, otherwise how would we have survived the bullies? They were nothing compared to the likes of Arthur and Tommy.

We all failed our eleven plus one by one and all ended up at Saint Thomas's Church School, Graisley Lane, now this is where all our training became worthwhile, Ron was there about a year and a half before me so was his reputation, 'Ronko' was his nickname, it was made up of the words Ron and k o which being the abbreviation for 'knock out', must admit it fitted very well. To the side of the school was an assembly room, it was called the Institute, it was a room where they forced us to attend roll-call, sing and pray to their god every morning before we set about our daily lessons, to the side of the assembly room was a long alley which led up a slight hill to an open park called King George's Playing Fields, about a quarter of a mile away. One sunny evening, coming out late from school class, hearing the roar of what seemed like a football crowd in the distance, the noise came from the direction we used to walk home, it grew louder and louder, my route was up the side of the Institute across the fields and past the Cottage Homes, the unwanted-kids home mentioned earlier, nearing the fields, from the hilltop one could see the whole panorama, the noise grew louder and louder and, on reaching the field, which was about half a mile square surrounded by iron railings in the middle, probably ninety present of the school were there shouting and screaming and in the middle of the crowd was a small open area with four kids obviously fighting, which one could see from a distance, forcing my way through the baying crowd, who should be in the middle but Ron and three others? Ron was holding his own against the three of them, his specs smashed and hanging off his face, with one earpiece missing, blood dripping from his nose, pushing my way through the crowd and wading in we stood back to back, like trained gladiators, we repelled them and we fought our causes without regret or shame. When Ron reached the age of fourteen he drifted away with his friends, but what was a friend to me? it was someone you could rely on to stab you in the front not in the back, up to that stage of my life having never met a good friend and at the age of twelve never imagined such a person existed, meanwhile my paper round paid twelve shillings a week of which Tommy took ten and also there was my job as a wringer-out for a one-armed window cleaner, just kidding, I used to collect the money for a window cleaner and Tommy never knew, I just wasted it on sweets and pop therefore developing toothache and deciding, after several weeks of pain, to visit the local dentist, when we were ill no one ever took us to the doctor or dentist we had to go ourselves, even at the age of six I made visits on my own, the doctor was only a short walk away and tonsillitis was one of my main problems, it was always too much trouble for Elsie to take us so we knew no different. The local dentist's name was Sanderson, his surgery was at Black Halve Lane about half a mile away, he also was a barrister part time, when going in to explain my problem and I was tempted to crack the old joke, 'raise your right hand and repeat after me, do you swear to pull the tooth the whole tooth and nothing but the tooth', I didn't and neither did he, he took out four teeth, well that's what he said. Upon arriving home and the cocaine wearing off, the pain was unbearable, Elsie said 'don't be such a baby it will go off,' so I stuck it out for about three weeks and only ate the liquid from Elsie's stews and any other sort of nourishment it was possible to eat, the pain was still unbearable, after three weeks so off back to the dentists, at the reception the person said 'yes,' I explained about these broken teeth in my gum from the previous visit, the pieces of jagged tooth were cutting my tongue, the receptionist went berserk, 'how dare you,' and abruptly said, 'make another appointment', tears of frustration ran down my face whilst standing my ground in sheer cool anger and refusing to leave, to defy authority in those days at such a young age was looked down upon, and if you had an opinion you were classed as a trouble maker, elders were always right and their response was always a clout, even from strangers, even the coppers would clout you in those days, upon hearing the commotion Sanderson came out and directed me to the dental room, after ten minutes he was done, then I went home with what seemed a thick lip and waited for the cocaine to wear off, when it did the relief was absolute, the pain had gone, just two holes where he had removed the broken teeth, a lesson was learned that day by me, at the age of twelve-and-a-half, to stand my ground no matter what.

Most school lessons were a drag - French lessons, art, woodwork, technical drawing and that was it for me - every year my school exam results were poor compared with Ron and Dianne, Tommy Davies used to threaten me to do as well as them, this gave me a false hope that he was concerned for my future, so knuckling under, studying, and concentrating was my goal, the other side of the coin would be the belt from Tommy, every year after my position got better in class, Ron and Di were usually first or second in the brains department with me about tenth or so, but we were all in A classes which was a top class. Some of the teachers at Saint Thomas's were sadistic, they had a system: ten credits, a badge and teachers pet; three debits, the cane (or the cosh as we nicknamed it). The credit or credits system was awarded for good work and a debit for bad work, it was not unusual to get five credits in one go on the one hand and get three debits in one go on the other, depending on the quality of your work and the sanity of the teacher, if you did amass three debits within a month it was six whacks of the cane on the arse, often to end up in the headmaster's study for 'six of the best' as they named it, Religious Instruction, Maths, Algebra and English had nothing to do with hands-on work so, being a regular visitor to the headmaster's study for that reason, it never bothered me, my mind was conditioned by Arthur and Tommy to withstand the blows, to show no pain although it hurt bad, often coming out of the study with my posterior stinging, walking past the queue of awaiting offenders, sometimes cracking a joke or doing something funny and, when they went in one by one for their punishment, it was worse for them because they were grinning and the head took it they were laughing at him and at his punishment, so when he whacked them he would stand on tippy-toe to administer the ultimate pain, looks like I have inherited a sadistic streak like my half-brother Arthur. We had a science teacher, his name was Barry Bough, boy was he sick in the head, he used to sit on his desk which was elevated above the rest of the class so he could rule from his seat of power like a Caesar, surveying all, in his hand he carried a powerful double-barrel popgun, it was his baton to rule, he would load it with corks or chalk and shoot at you whilst you were writing essays that he had set, hoping the distraction would make you make mistakes, which we all often did, how could we concentrate knowing a cork or piece of chalk was about to bounce off our heads? This was his excuse to punish certain pupils he had taken a dislike to, using the debit system to get you the cane for nothing. The first Indian lad who came to our school was called Gupta, Bough shouted him out in front of the science class, 'Gupta, come out here boy your lot can walk on hot coals,' he took a piece of phosphorous out of a jar of liquid with a pair of tongues, 'hold out your hand boy,' he said and proceeded to place the yellow tablet in the palm of Gupta's hand, the chalky-looking tablet started to wiz and fizz around giving out what looked like tremendous heat, all Gupta did was laugh his head off, 'Killer' as we had nicknamed Bough, was not very happy and gave him three across the hand with a secret cane he had hidden in his cupboard, was it some sort of trick or was it supposed to burn the flesh or did Killer know something we didn't? Surely Killer would not have risked his job being discovered by such an act, what was it that sent Killer on one of his ranting rages? Was it the fact that Gupta was supposed to retaliate in fear of being burned instead of laughing? If any scientific brains ever read this book it would be interesting to know. Another of Killer's favourite pastimes was to get a bowl of soapy water, take the hose off the Bunsen burner, immerse it in the soapy water turn on the gas, causing the bowl of soapy water to bubble, the bubbles would rise being filled with gas, eventually the large cloud of bubbly gas would rise in the air. There was a lad named Howard Katz, Killer shouts, 'Pussy, come out here' (he nicknamed us all), the poor lad was made to stand on top of the desk over the bowl and on Killer's command the victim was made to plunge a lighted taper into the cloud thus resulting in a ball of flame that often took your eyebrows off and some of your hair, then Killer would scream insanely, 'great balls of fire!' now come to think of it Killer's hair was styled the same as Gerry Lee Lewis and he wore his clothes with the same mannerisms, hence the reason some clever little swat had given him the nickname of Killer, he was as perverted as Lewis at the time, he used to corner the more voluptuous young girls, well one young girl in particular, and rub himself against her sexually. This man ruled the school with fear and that was how he got away with it, anyway no one would believe a minor above an adult, Killer hated the kids who were different and about this time the D.A. was coming into style for young lads along with Elvis, Cliff and such, short back and sides was the school code of appearance for boys. Killer would humiliate any boy who came into his class with the D.A, for those of you who don't know what the D.A. is, it was short for 'ducks arse', look at the back of a duck and there you have it, simple, nothing obtrusive, just a bit different. One of the days Ron was taking lessons in Killer's class, this story was told to me by his best mate Oswald Osborn, no not the infamous bat-eating one, just a lad with the same name, Killer calls Ron out, 'Wilfred,' he shouts to Ron, Ron ignores him, 'Wilfred!' he shouts again, agitated, Ron ignores him again, not being ignorant just not knowing who this Wilfred was because Killer had just invented it as a form of humiliation. 'You Davies, with the musicians hair, come out here boy,' Ron looks up, 'you are cock of the school, Davies,' Killer says, 'when were you last at the barber's boy?' and then proceeded to try to tie a ribbon in Ron's hair. Big mistake, Ron gives him a look that could kill and snatches the ribbon out of his hair and throws it in Killer's face, the blood enters Killer's neck and head and he goes bright red with rage, goes straight to the cupboard for the secret cane and brandishes it, Ron snatches it off Killer and snaps it in half, 'ten debit's!' Killer rants, 'ten debit's, off - to the headmaster for the cane!' he screams, Ron looks him straight in the face and says, 'NO'. That day Killer lost his reign of terror over the school.

Killer used to stand in for maths lessons, one particular day when sitting directly behind a lad named Warburton - come to think of it this lad was a bit of a Jonah to me, a bad omen - who was doing something he should not, Killer whacked the board rubber at him, this was a block of wood about two inches by four inches with a piece of felt stuck on the bottom for cleaning the blackboard, Warburton ducked and the wood hit me straight in the face, the blood poured and Killer panicked, begging me not to say anything and promising to let me get away with any future misconduct but maybe this was a spin-off from Ron's confrontation, from that day on he never picked on me ever again, when eventually Killer did leave the school, he got a job teaching kids at Borstal Approved school, with me hoping one of them would be my half-brother Barry. Now, to get back to this lad Warburton, if you conjure the name Warburton in your head you will probably realize it's the name of a popular loaf of British bread and the French for bread is *pain* pronounced 'pan', and this Warburton was a pain to me not only on the head but also in my *derrière*, as Del-Boy might say, one time when taking my French exams this Pain sat in front of me, again by coincidence, my French was excellent so I finished my paper well before the end of time, Warburton turned round to me and asked, 'have you finished?' to which my reply was, 'yes', but in that nanosecond my French teacher must have looked up and in that nano of a nano-second must have seen the moment when the word 'yes' came from my mouth, hence the movement of my mouth, And he marked me as a cheat, and I was called out to bring my paper to the teacher's desk, he promptly ripped up my paper denoting me as a cheat to the rest of the class, he gave me a blank paper in return and with ten minutes left he said, 'do it again', well five minutes was enough, it was easy to me and no harm done, the thing was, for top marks in the exam the school often awarded a top prize and, ironically, for some reason this was given to Warburton, it was a book on French cooking and I had been thinking of giving it to Elsie because her cooking was pretty similar to a French peasants - horrible.

By 1960 Ron was fourteen-and-a-half, and Dianne was fifteen-and-a-half, this pleased Tommy because work was looming for them and Tommy could reap the benefits of wages coming into the house, but little did he realize that a revolution was coming as well, a new style of life and new ideals with the brilliant youth of England heading the renaissance, even at my age of twelve you could feel the energy, everything is possible when seen through the eyes of youth and we were shaking off the chains of discontent, we knew that it was going to be a brilliant era to live in, or we thought so, no doubt there was a place for me in this new world which was buzzing with artistic talent and ideas and I was bursting to lay myself bare to the world. Dianne left school and went to night school to learn shorthand and typing from which she got a secretarial job at Guy Motors which was one of the main companies in the area, we still lived in a filthy house so we started to clean it on a regular basis, having visited other kid's houses for the first time and seen how clean they were and we owed it to ourselves to do so, we washed, ironed and repaired our own clothes, sewed and darned any buttons back that went missing, we made sure we kept ourselves washed and clean because head lice were prevalent in most schools, although when most kids were given a letter from the nit nurse to take home they thought it something special and it was much to the shame of their parents. We scrubbed and washed the flea-ridden bedroom we slept in, often with odd looks from Tommy, and we had a paper round each again so we could spend some money on ourselves, unknown to Tommy of course because we kept it secret, he still had his mannerisms and crudeness and it was starting to irritate, you see the child was starting to become the man and the influence of the Sixties was starting to take effect, the mental subjection of living in the house of depression was being lifted, music was filling our hearts and minds and those early pioneers of rock & roll will never realize how much we, the working class, owe to them, for they were the ones who awoke us from the deep sleep of the depression of our rusty past to cast the revolution in the foundries of our minds that gave birth to the Sixties.

A few months later Dianne started a catalogue, Kay's it was called, it was amazing what you could get for a few shillings a week so we bought our own modern clothes and shoes for school, also casual wear, and the catalogue made a change from a provident cheque, which all the poor got, a kind- of money lender would supply it and you had to pay interest on it weekly, it was called the 'never-never' because you were never, never out of debt, you had to present the provident cheque to a shop called the Red House in Wolverhampton where all the poor went, sometimes you could buy stuff cheap from an Army and Navy stores, the trouble was, some of the poorer kids would attend school dressed as Jap Snipers or Kamikaze Pilots, it would have suited Tommy if we had done the same had we not purchased our own, it was embarrassing for kids to attend school in weird clothes because then everyone knew they were poor which was a stigma in those days to most people who still had a sense of pride, true the provident system was similar to the catalogue but with the catalogue you shopped in the book and the clothes were posted to you so no one knew where they came from. The catalogue opened up our world to modern fashion and colour instead of the drab, grey, cloth-cap, belt-'n-bracers image that surrounded the Black Country at the time and, as anyone knows, clothes help you express yourself.

There was only one time in Elsie's life that I ever saw her doubt the faith in her faith - the rented property we lived in was to be sold, the landlord, who was the brother of Sammy Lewis the owner of the paper shop, told her he was selling up his properties so we either had to get out or purchase, I often came home from school to find Elsie with head in hands worried by the dilemma, she told me she needed £900 to purchase the house which in those times was unobtainable for us working classes, but mom was like me, at the time she never fully realised the power of the gift that she preached and gave, she had done the football pools for years and never won a thing, the night we sat together and joined our hands we felt the strange energy between us, just thought it was love but it was more than that it was a more sublime power, the next day was Saturday, the following evening coming home to a buzzing sensation surrounding the house, a feeling of happiness and joy upon entering the door, 'I've won!' Mom screams, 'I've won the pools', sure enough she had won just under £1000 pounds, a gift from the seventh-born?

2.

Madness

We neared school-leaving age, Ron asked Elsie and Tommy if he could serve an apprenticeship at the Steel Tube, a local factory where most school leavers went, it was expected you would end up doing some menial job in a working class environment for the rest of your drab life, they said yes, this was to make a career for him, it was a five-year apprenticeship in a boring steel-tube foundry far below the intellect of Ron, anyway he stayed the five years and gained some decent friends but not much skill except how to make steel tubes, Ron, like me, was more a leader than an obeyer, we drifted apart over those years and we often fought each other over minor things, we were about to take our different paths in life, by this time at the age of fourteen-and-a-half, still at school and hanging around with lads in small gangs on street corners, not making trouble, it was just that they all had motorcycles that their parents had paid for and it was possible to cadge a lift to Bridgnorth every now and then which was the local Sunday run, I was starting to ignore and disregard authority at school and often turned up in a leather jacket defying anyone to dispute it but they never did. A youth club was started at the school, this was designed to keep young kids like me off the streets, I found it interesting and took a hand in helping to set it up, there was a coffee bar which I helped make at woodwork along with other pieces of furniture, the club was like Happy Days with me in my leather jacket and denim jeans and the rest of the morons in twin sets - like the clothes Andy Williams and Perry Como wore at the time - probably what the morons' mothers had bought them, their favourite music was Ray Charles, Bing Crosby, Matt Monroe, to me this music was boring and uninteresting, the latest from Radio Caroline was my bag, often listening to it on my small crystal radio-set, bought from the catalogue as was my leather jacket, after a while the youth club became boring too, they were all embarrassing to me, Tommy would say, 'what a load of 'ponces,' which he interpreted as meaning 'Nancy boys', but if you take the word *ponceuse* from the French it means 'smooth' so he even got that wrong. Meanwhile after working hard all year and finishing my final term second in the class and due to leave school, and needing to find a career, it was easy for me to choose - anything hands-on, with a distinction in art tucked under my arm, which in today's terms is an A level, the picture that got me through was of Tommy painted by me to depict cruelty, my art teacher said hanging would be good for him, I agreed. My art teacher suggested art school, being able to put my hand to anything such as joinery or technical drawing and my French reading and writing were perfect for my age, with high marks in all these subjects. 'Right art school, that's the way to create a brilliant future for myself.' With all my four years of results under my arm, proud to confront Elsie and Tommy as Ron and Dianne had done before me, told them of my hopes. 'Oh no yo Dow,' Tommy sneers, 'one on yow as gorra bring sum munny in the arse, yow con gew and get a propa job, bay keepin yow an all'. A proper job in his mind, was manual work, cheap labour and such, and to my dismay Elsie never fought my corner as she did for Ron and Dianne, so there it was, the first thought that came to my head was why did you punish me and torture me over those years when my school work was poor giving me false hope that you cared? What was the point? What was in your head - revenge? Revenge for what? From that day the certainty came to me that Tommy Davies hated me, and I don't know why even to this day, there was something in my past or my mother's past that haunted him, there was a catalyst that poisoned him towards me, you will find out before the end of this book, then the dark secret can be revealed. One thing David told me was that Elsie once told him of the time in 1946, when Tommy buggered off with another woman, to turn up on her doorstep at a later time with his 'floozy' as Elsie called her, and Tommy said he was moving in with her, David said Elsie slammed the door in their faces and they left, you can work out there was a period of about eighteen months when Tommy was not on the scene, and this was the time when I arrived. But from where? There's no z-shaped scar on my head, maybe there's a six-six-six, under my hairline, garlic is quite nice and argent doesn't bother me, but what is it, what is the secret, what is the dammed secret?

You know, although being very streetwise, when it came for me to find a job this was a totally new ball game, it was me versus it, without a clue, no insider to vouch for me, no one to advise me how to go about earning a living, the school career's officer might as well have stamped 'reject' on my forehead for all the good his advice was, he seemed to think warehouse work would suit me, after a few weeks of nagging sarcasm from Tommy telling people, that I was idle and no good, he could not understand that I wanted to better myself, that I didn't want to spend the rest of my days behind a machine, there was too much going on inside my head, anyway Dianne stepped in. 'Come to Guy Motors and start as an apprentice in the drawing office, I will get you an interview,' she said. Dianne had been there a couple of years, she was dating a bloke in the drawing office, a good idea it seemed to me at the time, it would keep Tommy off my back and, excelling at technical drawing at school, there was a possibility of becoming a draughtsman and that was a start. The next day Dianne made an appointment for me to see the career's officer at Guys. 'You will have to do six months on the shop floor,' he said, 'before we will consider you,' more fool me for gladly accepting, my future was going to be a draughtsman all right but someone who opens and shuts doors to keep the draft out for the rest of my life, nevertheless I started work optimistically the following week for one pound fifteen shillings a week for a forty-hour week, learning to operate certain machines, it was a filthy job, gallons of slurry turned me into a spotty urk, the slurry was white oil used to cool the hot steel on the lathes and it flowed constantly, splashing everywhere, for me to end up making washers all day long, my artistic fingers cut to pieces fending off the long strings of hot swarf ever spiralling towards me, matter of fact still have pieces of metal embedded in my fingers from those days, a poignant reminder of how boring my life was. The six months passed, nothing happened so off to the main office to ask about my promised apprenticeship as a draughtsman, 'there are no opportunities yet,' was the reply, 'when they arrive we will let you know,' eighteen months later still putting grooves in washers for one pound fifteen shillings a week of which Tommy took one pound twenty five for my keep. It was about this time that J.F.K. was messing about with the Russians and he was telling us in the west we had to take action to save democracy - the Cuba Missile Crisis was what they called it - he and Khrushchev were playing Russian roulette with our lives. The final showdown came at high noon, I stood in that filthy factory with many others, the sword of Damocles hanging over our heads, waiting for my end just to satisfy someone else's ego, never to forgive or forget the trauma of a fifteen-year-old lad who had not even tasted the life to come, that day Lee Harvey Oswald was blamed for shooting Kennedy's brains out, Elsie's philosophy came to mind, it did not matter to me who pulled the trigger because I was sure Kennedy and his Generals would have eventually led us into a third world war. According to my sister-in-law, Marlene, Kennedy once told the German race, '*ich bin ein Berliner*', which in German meant he was a doughnut, how appropriate, could not agree more, so he was a laughing stock to the German race too, as you can see there is no time in my life for murderers and killers in the name of humanity, and any time justice is handed out I applaud my mother who spoke the word of it. This crisis made me realize the value of life when about to lose it and life is valued above all things by me. 'Right, sod it, no more working for nothing as a cheap labourer doing the same job as a married bloke who was getting fifteen pounds a week'. But alas, from then on I drifted from job to job doing menial work, putting threads on bolts, counting nuts and washers and other boring tasks, just to get some money to eat and live, but with poor wages people used me, being young and vulnerable and on my own, there were many jobs like this, a job came up at one particular small family factory which employed about ten staff, a back-street dirt-floor Dickensian-type factory, one could say a place of Great Expectations for me, some of the machines were originally belt-driven by a steam engine and had been modified but were still out of date, without any unions to protect you and stand up for your rights as a human being, the owners could treat you like a convict which they often did, and for anyone to dispute a decision or have an opinion was classed as a sin to these church-going, godly people, the boss of the firm said to me one morning, 'make the tea, boy'. 'Where's the tea pot and where are the cups?' was my reply. 'What?' he said with a discerning look on his face. 'Where are the cups and tea pot?' I repeated. 'Sir to me,' he said, 'you say sir to me, boy' whilst twisting my ear. Needless to say, me and my rebellious ways told him to get stuffed, I took a swipe at him and he sacked me on the spot, one week later going to the office for the four days' wages they owed me from the previous week - because you always worked a week in hand and in those days it was always in their hand - the boss refused to pay me, told me to go beg for my money, picking up one of the wage packets lying on the desk, waved it in front of his face and said, 'this will do' and walked out, needless to say the police came to the house a few hours later and eventually sent me to court for stealing someone else's wages and I got two years' probation for it, that was the only

Pete Davies

time in my life I did wrong in the eyes of the law, but in my eyes I did completely right by standing up for myself, but now I was the third criminal in the family: there was one who killed a rabbit to eat, one who peddled a bike on the pavement and one who claimed his own wages and stuck up for his rights, what a rogues' gallery. I was the sort of person who would have been shipped to the colonies a hundred years earlier and classed as another criminal undesirable, but to me all those criminal undesirables are my brothers and sisters, people who stood up for theirselves, most times just to survive, but they were no good to a system that relies on conformity and weakness to function, in the court rooms of England the inhuman judges sounded their gavels to show they were strong and that the laws were decisive and equal, to show that the strings of the deeply-distinguished, judicious wigs and cloaks could not be pulled or persuaded, making examples of the poor and the hungry. Looking suspicious or having an opinion were serious enough crimes to get you deported, those English outcasts have built a great country from nothing, no wonder the Australians don't like the way they were mistreated even to this day, by the way they never paid me the wages they owed me so who was the thief?

From then on my early working life was paralleled by my school life, always problems and disastrous, once I obtained a job working for the council and at the time their policy was to employ so many disabled persons and my first assistant was a one-armed labourer whose job consisted of pushing a cart to its destination by hand, loaded with materials needed for the day's work. After talking to myself for several minutes I turned around and the one-armed man was going around in circles with the cart at the top of the road in complete silence, I walked back, 'what's up,' I said, 'can't steer it with one arm,' he says, it was me who ended up pushing the cart to its destination with him sitting on the end of it. Upon arrival at the job, 'okay, put the ladder up,' I said. 'Can't,' he said. 'Why?' I said. 'Only have one arm,' he said. So, after erecting the ladder, 'right, mix some compo,' I said. 'Can't,' he said, 'can't hold the shovel'. After mixing the cement with him standing over me, watching me put it in the bucket, 'there you go,' I said, 'bring it up the ladder.' 'Can't,' he said, 'it's not possible for me to hold the bucket and climb the ladder at the same time.' Up the ladder I go with the bucket. 'Clean the place up then,' I said. 'Can't,' he said, 'can't hold the broom?' Finishing the job, I cleaned up, got the ladder down and wheeled the cart back to the depot completely knackered and him fit as a fiddle, after five days as a wet nurse payday arrived and there was not a bad bonus for a week's work. 'Come into the office,' the boss says, 'there is a complaint, your labourer wants equal rights so you will have to split your bonus.' I tried to explain my situation but to no avail, they made me feel guilty, said I was inconsiderate, even lucky to have a job, said they were obliged to employ him because he'd lost his arm during a fight at work with another labourer and they were responsible, I was seething mad and said, 'well, give me the winner.' They gave me the sack instead, for lack of compassion. The next job to come my way was the same sort of thing but without the cripple, well not quite, working with a labourer who was a Teddy boy, sort-of crippled in the mind, to attend work he wore a blue velvet suit with black velvet collar, string tie, silk shirt and brothel creepers, his tool kit consisted of one comb, one chain and one flick hammer, mentally he always seemed to have something cooking but nothing in the pan, he brushed himself down at every speck of dust, he was a kind of gentleman Ted. Whilst working by a row of shops this jitterbugging Ted disappeared for an hour to return some time later smoking and eating, the next day I was called into the office, ' we have had a complaint, the police have been notified, what have you done with the money?' 'What money?' was my reply. 'We know it's you, the Teddy boy said so!' Apparently some money had been taken from a jar in one of the shops near to where we had worked, and I had done it - result, sack. Next week an apology came through the post, the police had been informed that a person dressed as a Ted had been to the paper shop in the same row of shops on the same day the missing money was discovered and had purchased twenty fags and a pork pie, all in pennies and halfpennies, they never offered me my job back and I was left singing the blues. Everything up to that point in my life seemed like a trial of patience, and all it ever seemed is that it was me that got judged for other peoples actions, 'why is it me who always gets burdened by fools,' I would ask myself, I seemed to be carrying the weight of responsibility for those I did not know, were these trials the trials of life that were preached to me at an early age when at school praying at the institute, the so called trials given to us so we can be judged when judgement day does come? Putting that seed of doubt in my mind, that there is a special place awaiting us all depending on our actions on this world. Often people say, 'why me', some may say these trials are a test of faith from your god to find your strengths and weaknesses, or do those ideas just come from scheming people taking advantage of a situation? Mom warned me of these ridiculous ideals and the trials and tribulations of life, is this book her message although written by me, sent to you like a full stop, a comma, a question mark, in the story of life, a thinking point, a small rest designed to make you stop and think? These stories may seem funny but that is because they have been dipped in sugar, strip them down and inside there is a real message with one commandment: 'be true to yourself'. Tommy Davies, armed with all this, gave me grief, the thought of going back home any more with the prospect of no job, no money and, eventually, nowhere to live, was nightmarish, the only way for me and probably many other kids in my situation was to join the army, it was impossible to get lodgings on such poor pay even with a job. The other option was to end up living on the street or robbing a bank, and I didn't fancy Australia, so it was off to the recruitment offices unknown to anyone, I did the interview but was refused entry due to my probation order, they said, 'come back when you are clear'. In my later years when working on those army camps many of the old soldiers spoke of the luxury of being issued with underwear, the facilities and security the armed forces offered, and, let's face it, to go to a foreign country was an exciting prospect for any working class lad in those days. On the other hand, in later years, whilst doing a contract working for various army camps in the area and when using the N.A.A.F.I. for breakfast, to see the tears in some of the young recruits' eyes, desperate for their parents to buy them out of their situation, was heart-breaking, to fit in the armed forces you have to be tough before you go in, there's no point going into the forces if you are a mummy's boy unless you are a commissioned officer, the army would not have suited me, it would have been hard for me to take the discipline or be stripped of my personality to be rebuilt to someone else's specification, which is what the army has to do in order for you to function on the battlefield, we often read of our love for our fellow man, to me it's like brotherly love, does it really exist? All brothers and sisters fight on occasion but the thing is, blood is thicker than water and if confronted with a choice between family and others, others will always get it, the same with a patriot no matter what, it's a pack thing, you see it in all animals and humans are animals, and this is why they at times choose to kill each other, they have ceremonies to remember their dead from all wars, but so do the people they fight against whom they are sometimes taught to hate and from an early age. None of them want to fight and die, some people will say those brave people died so that you can do what you are doing now, but ask yourself what are you doing now? What will you be doing in five years - the same thing, and our soldiers will still be fighting these pointless wars, well you cannot even call them wars. Times have changed, they don't need to police other countries, let those warring countries sort their own problems out, after all we are an island with a defensive moat. Bring all our soldiers home to aid the police and the customs service, think of the massive amounts of money our nation would save, the brilliant security system we would have. Till someone stands up in our government with courage and conviction, brave men and families will still be paying the ultimate price and still no one will be listening. It was one of your greatest leaders that said meeting jaw to jaw is better than war, and no one listened to him either.

I heard that there were some lucrative jobs going at Goodyear's where Tommy Davies worked, a job where it was possible to save, go to college and still leave enough money to get lodgings, attending the interview I got the job, as usual starting at the bottom of the queue in the repairs department, *i.e.* mending inner tubes with patches, what a lousy job but the prospects were good, the wages could be thirty pounds a week once one of the better jobs came up. The head of the department was a bloke named Charlie Blower, a name often mentioned by Tommy Davies around the house, Charlie Blower this, Charlie Blower that, and by the tone of Tommy's voice you could tell they were mates, the bad news was, on the first day of that rotten job Tommy Davies was in Charlie Blower's office and they were looking my way, this seemed very odd to me because it was the first time I ever saw Tommy Davies talk to anyone outside the family and, come to think of it, the first time I saw anyone outside our house talk to him, the time passed and six months went by with me still mending tubes although young lads were coming into the department and going on to more lucrative jobs, with me stuck there in limbo amongst the incapable ones, the ones who had no ambition and were basically backward. After twelve months, madness and boredom were taking over my mind, I decided to confront Charlie Blower. After knocking on the office door, 'come in,' he said, Charlie was sitting there, his big fat paunch hanging over his belt. 'Well?'

he said. 'Why is it that people come in for a few weeks, go on to better jobs, and I am stuck here?' 'We need you here for the time being,' was the reply, and me, being gullible, believed him and his lies, my life was taking a massive dive into despair, working shifts for as little as six pounds a week of which Tommy had four, leaving me two pounds a week, this was all that was left to feed and clothe myself, and there was also my social life which was near zero. By this time seventeen years of age was looming with no prospects whatsoever, then one day out of the darkness shone a light, talking to Ron later that same day he said. 'Have you heard this band they are called the Beatles,' and they were singing a song called *Please, Please Me*, that band changed my life, it was the first time I heard them and I immediately knew they would be bigger than Elvis, I loved the John Lennon stance of arrogance and the power that fame had given him, some of the songs John wrote paralleled parts of my life, John in later years said, 'they are just songs and if they fit your situation, well that's okay'. The haunting song *Mother* I would take to mean Mother Earth, the opening line, 'Mother you had me I never had you' was symbolic of my life at the time, knowing there was a reason for me to be here and not knowing why, *Happy Xmas War Is Over* was to me the most depressing Christmas song ever but glad he called it 'Xmas' because to me that is what it is, nothing, denoted by the 'X', such a negative letter, 'And So This Is Christmas', the opening lines of that nagging song, was a message from John which came to me every year, asking me what had I done. There was something for me to do, it was frustrating not knowing what it was and at that time I had done nothing worthwhile in my life, now there's a good title for a song. The day John was killed devastated me like many others, to me the person who died that day was someone who spoke and said what he thought, which is very rare even in these days, some might say you never knew John Lennon, no, but we all knew of him, he had a dream and a belief and a style, he was bursting with talent and no one, no matter who, could contain that because that was him. In order to progress you have to ignore standard life procedures, John knew he had betrayed himself and his music, but no one could ever tell him for fear of his acid tongue and sharp wit, anyway, he would never have discussed it with anyone, it was his and his alone to deal with, and that's my opinion, and only my opinion, not influenced by anyone else's opinion, just the opinion of a seventh-born.

Meanwhile Tommy Davies still dominated, but his days of terror were coming to an end, we were starting to overtake him in stature and my fear of him had gone and to me he was nothing. Remember the time of taking bets for Tommy Davies, running the gauntlet through the Scotland's? Well later on, at the age of thirteen or so, my newspaper round was in the same area, and the same happened when delivering the papers and I'm sure the bullies were the same ones, but they had grown to become thugs, they still intimidated me, outnumbering me ten to one they managed to split my lip or tear some part of my clothing even up to the age of fifteen, the point is, about a couple of years later an old school mate came to my house, Stuart was his name, and he asked me if it was possible to help him out because he was being bullied by a gang from the Scotland's, they would be waiting for him on neutral ground. Lo and behold, sitting on the wall of Stuart's house with his gang was this thug who had been one of my main persecutors over the years, I walked over to him ignoring his mates, faced him square on, 'do you remember me, you used to beat me when a defenceless kid?' The blood drained from his face. In more ways than one, I could have sworn that even my guardian angel removed his halo and blessed him with a gypsy's kiss and put the sandal in as well. Was this the justice that Elsie talked of? No, it was my justice and mine alone, my satisfaction, my glory, my contentment and my personal revenge, sometimes it's hard to wait for fate or even the law to take its part, which we often don't see - and sometimes there's satisfaction dishing out one's own justice. It was November 1964 when *Beatles For Sale,* the record, came out, it was a wake-up call to me like a hidden message, I listened to it one drab, dark November evening wondering where was my life going, thinking to myself, if only it was possible to meet someone decent for a change, someone to talk to, someone on my wave length, if any such person existed, I was sick of the school morons who were sentenced to the factory for life, buying a motorcycle on the strap and paying forever, polishing it at a weekend, talking about bikes as though they were people, my brain needed more and it could not stand those two-faced so-called friends, two months later, January 1965, visiting my old youth club out of sheer boredom, I sat in the corner of the room, fag in mouth, playing cards with a couple of lads, and looked up and across the room, mixed amongst others, there were three girls, they were all dressed the same in the trendy modern clothes of the time, in the style of an American girl soul group, this immediately caught my eye and my attention, at last someone with an imagination, and none of them resembled Olive Oil, Popeye's girlfriend, and none of them dressed like their mothers with a coat and head scarf and curlers beneath, my attention was distracted, my brain cried out for more, one of them was caked with makeup like a drag queen, the other one was just plain ugly but my eye caught the last girl with her back to me, when she turned round she was the prettiest girl ever, my eyes were transfixed, she must have sent my hormones racing, my mind said to me, 'get up go over there and speak to her'. This was a first to me because she was a complete stranger, I walked straight across the room and touched her by her arm to attract her attention and said, 'hello never seen you here before'. Now, wait a minute, from this point on everything has to be perfectly right because I will stand corrected if it isn't - not only was she pretty, she was straight talking and interesting, not in an academic way, she had this thing and still has, don't ask me what it is, maybe it's a spell cast on me by myself on that cold November night, but she is me and I was under that spell. There's a certain kind of light that burns in some people, let's say a contentment with their being, they know within themselves that they are pure of mind and that they need to feel no remorse for things they have procured in their lives, they are the ones that make life worth living, the bearable ones, you may meet one in your lifetime, two if you are lucky, they exist and they are the special ones. Contentment comes not from possession, wealth, riches or circumstance; certainly it cannot come from the pressures to be good in this life in fear of what may come after death. We are all told we are free to choose our own path in this life, try to find a quiet empty place, shut everything out from your world, a calmness may come to you, in a kind of meditation, the same way I would sit as a kid when locked away for days, try to think of what you are, what you aspire to be, and where you are going in this life, ask these questions of yourself and work it out, you will not be pure in thought but you will see, try to remove the barriers and the pressures of people and life, relax the mind and go back to when all was well and good and start from there, it may just be a fleeting moment of joy that enters your head, in my case it would be the sunny days Ron and I would sit on the dirt floor behind the air-raid shelter bathed in the early morning sun, hidden from Tommy, with my favourite book of the time in hand. You may start to feel the flicker of contentment pointing you to the direction you desire, open the doors to your mind and try it, what have you got to lose? When asked the secret of a long marriage or partnership, call it what you want, many people don't know the answer, to me the answer is always: stick together, never let anything or any person drive a wedge between the two of you, if your partner smokes or drinks and you don't, so what, don't try to change a person to suit your own needs, it won't work, many times the one partner quits a habit and smugly grinds the other to paste, humiliating them at every opportunity and sometimes in front of complete strangers, this spells disaster, true, no matter what, no two people can ever see eye to eye continually. Individuality is what makes an interesting person not predictability, predictability only breeds boredom. The soldier who fights with me is a complete opposite to me, caring, loving and helpful, and good-looking at times, me, I'm negative in a positive sort of way and Jean is a positive in a negative sort of way. Many challenges on the road through life will arise, some will try to divide you because they want what you have got, when we first met, Jean had been told many times by so called friends of hers and mine that I was a waster, a no-conformer, different to others, someone who would not go quietly, but that was just dirt of gossip and the dust of rumours by people who didn't even know me, they saw the surface and judged me from rumours which they didn't know the reason for just like Elsie had warned me in her prophecy, years after, even Geoff Green, Dianne's first husband after his divorce from Dianne, went to Woolworth's where Jean worked and told her to steer clear of me, me! the only one who had sympathized with him after their marriage break-up, had gone with him to the pub though never liking lager or pubs at that time - because lager tastes like liquid privet hedge and people can be irritating when sober never mind when drunk - me! the one who gave him support and consoled him when he was low, alone and suicidal, gave him my time, kept him informed of the goings on - for what? To be stabbed in the back. These are the sort of people who destroy marriages and people's lives. At the end of the day, he was a miserable boring bloke and Dianne wanted a life, that's the top and bottom of it, she latched on to this younger bloke who liked fun. Forty odd years Jean and I have been together so we know what we're saying, we still have our own opinions, sometimes they escalate into arguments but that's all they are, differences of opinion, it's good to keep a relationship

Pete Davies

interesting because when you argue it's a sign there is still fire in the relationship, it's when couples stop talking, stop having opinions and just listen to others, this is when the death knell tolls and the flame begins to diminish, these rules apply to everything, love, peace and war.

We talked for a while in the youth club and arranged to meet outside the local pub, the first night she never turned up, a week passed and we met again, 'how come you never turned up?' She replied, 'well at school you were a rebel, kicking doors and smoking and you had a bad reputation and I just thought you were taking the mick,' was this me she was talking about? True there was a chip on my shoulder, the world was a bastard and it was me versus it. Jean Sutton was her name and funny enough, her mother's maiden name was Sutton, her father's name was Sutton, of course, and Elsie's maiden name was Sutton, Jean's nick name at school was sooty, so she was my sooty and I was her sweep. We started seeing each other on a regular basis and no one else existed, it was 1966 and Cassius Clay was knocking out boxers left, right and centre, I was still knocking out inner tubes out at Goodyear's, England had just won the World Cup and we got our revenge on the Germans for causing the war, never on the field of football was so much owed by so many to so few, we out-fought the Germans on the pitch, in the goal and in the air, we never gave in, Winston may have encouraged it, even said it - but I never saw him there! Ron had finished his apprentice at the Steel Tube; he came home on the Friday night with just his wages to his name, went upstairs and started packing a bag. 'What are you doing Ron?' 'Leaving this miserable place, along with that miserable job,' was his retort. 'Where are you going?' 'Marrakesh,' was the answer, what a change to his personality, we said our goodbyes and he left that night, never saw him again for two years, he struggled whilst over there at various times from the letters he wrote to Elsie, but to my mind he did the right thing, meanwhile a few months later Tommy had changed his tactics from violent to the psychological, he had been weaving his web, conspiring with Charlie Blower to keep me so as not to progress and earn decent money at work, how sick is that? Not only that, he worked with another Davies who was married to Jean's mother's sister, he spun some tale about me, omitting reasons, and told this Davies about my probation order and obviously this got back to Jean's dad, we did not care, it would not break us, we took all the flack although it made life very difficult.

The Swinging Sixties were in full swing for some, someone once said, 'if you remember the Sixties you were not there,' that was probably just a wild drug-oriented statement from someone who was well enough off to upgrade from fags and beer to drugs and bubbly and probably doesn't even remember anything about the Sixties because they were permanently out of their tree and weren't there mentally for years, and probably some of the reasons people tend to see god at times after messing about with their genetic makeup, probably doesn't remember going to work either because they did not have to, the bank of mom and dad more than likely paid for it all, and then they progressed through life as hippies with free love and with their drug-addled brains and ideals, so confused that when they bred they created the birth of a new race, born to the Seventies, with the body of a man and the mind of a woman, as for me, never have taken any illegal substance in my life and never will, it's just a way of turning your back on responsibility, shutting yourself off from boredom and your unhappy situation, trouble is you have to come back to whatever sent you there in the first place, the only L.S.D. that interested me was of the monetary kind, to finance my dreams of reality. When about to leave the house to go out one night a shadow appeared behind the glass of the back door, upon opening it there before me was an absolute clone of Jimmy Hendrix, kaftan, coloured shirt, hairstyle, a deep suntan to his skin and not created by a tin of creosote or some stain or other, he had the lot, this stranger said to me in the poshest voice, 'hello Pete', no it wasn't my long lost dad, it was Ron, you could tell he had got himself a reasonable job because he had some money, trouble was, he also had a nervous breakdown somewhere along the line and, coupled with a few influences from others and probably a few chemicals, had turned into a born-again Christian and seen the light, to me religion is all tunnel vision, trouble with that light at the end of that tunnel is, it's sometimes a train coming the other way, anyway, he prays for me regularly, says I'm a sinner in his eyes, but it all depends on what you believe, maybe he's a sinner in my eyes for believing what he has read and not what he has seen and done. Meanwhile the Americans were planning the so-called Moon Landing, they had to try to beat the Russians who were playing up after they lost their little game of thermo-nuclear war and were now trying the psychological approach, trying constantly to intimidate the likes of Ron and me with their displays of power at the Kremlin and Red Square with their cardboard cut-outs similar to the Air-Fix model kits we used to build as kids only bigger, Ron and I would have beaten the Russians into space ten years earlier but we could not find a bottle big enough for the stick and we never used the correct glue, the Germans invented a flying bomb in the war and Elsie said some Nazi bugger had polished them so the spitfire pilots always had difficulty seeing them against the sun, the Americans borrowed the plans and the scientists and built a bigger one, you didn't need a bottle either, they just stood it upright, propped it against a scaffold, pointed it away from the earth, lit the fuse with a giant lighter and, whoosh, thousands of tons of rocket fuel jammed into a tube with only one way to go, upwards, they took off the warhead and replaced it with a tin can with three blokes in it, even to this day many doubt the event of the moon landings, some say it was just the Americans with their hands in their pockets trying to prove to the Russians who had got the biggest sputniks, with me sitting up all night like millions of others, watching and wondering in awe how the clever bugger got there first to set up the camera. J.F.K. once said, 'ask not what your country can do for you, ask, what you can do for your country', most people are sick of doing and dying for their countries and times have changed and now we need help from our countries, the politicians seem to have abandoned us and who else can we turn to in these stressful times, you can only give up so much without getting something back in return, when Abe Lincoln said, 'you can fool all of the people some of the time, and some of the people all, of the time, but you cannot fool all of the people all the time', that was a statement not a bloody order!

It was 1969, the Beatles had got bored with each other, Dylan had changed his tune, and Flower Power had arrived, trouble was most of the flowers were pansies, oh, and Jean decided we would get married. Tommy was still Tommy, he punched Ron in the face for having an opinion and blood poured everywhere but Ron never retaliated, he probably had to turn the other cheek due to his beliefs, Tommy came at me with a hammer a short time after that but I stood my ground and was ready to take the hammer from him but, like all bullies when confronted on their own, face to face, that's all they are, take the toughest out first and the rest will run, you may get a split lip or a black eye but your tormentor will never come back for more, in those days hardly anyone carried a weapon to bolster their courage but obviously Tommy felt the need. On the 21st March 1970, dumping our past life, Jean and I got married and began our new life and our rebirth, we rented a private flat and went about creating a secure future for ourselves without the burden of all that past, to us it was the past, just another of the seven levels of man, at first we struggled and we could not afford the flat we rented although we were both working, the wages were that bad, we sat once with one pound in our pockets amongst a stream of people in a shopping mall, armed only with one of Elsie's philosophies, which was - the harder you work the luckier you get. We dumped the flat also and went into lodgings, we worked all hours, dragged into the trap of democracy with me doing casual work, anything to bring in money on weekends and in the evenings after my day job, doing any odd job that people wanted me to do, even cleaning sewers and drains, removing toilet blockages, roof tiling and chimney repairs, dancing across roofs to replace an odd slate with no safety harness or suchlike device, risking severe injury or even death, just for a few bob, they were all jobs no one else wanted to do, eventually I became a master at the trade and was able to earn a reasonable living, then to form a gang of bricklayers and trawled the sites for work building houses and offices, there were many jobs in those days it was easy to get work and I would flitter from job to job like a cabbage white in a vegetable patch. Then Jean became pregnant with Martin, our only son, and this changed the state of play, a more stable income was needed, in other words a wage coming in every week. British Steel in Bilston were looking for furnace bricklayers and there was not much difference between what is called 'wet work' to 'dry stack', anyway they were prepared to train me, it was like laying bricks without cement, in the interview they had a film show of the dangers involved, burned bodies, people cut in half on the railway tracks, similar to a scene from Dante's inferno, in the factory black shadows of the damned were cast against the background of the fiery furnaces and when they rodded the liquid-iron showers of molten steel and metal, smoke and choking fumes polluted the graveyard at the rear of the factory where stood the giant ingots that had claimed the bodies of people who had fallen into the molten vats of steel to be pushed under to speed their deaths, one of the workers told me of the story of a father and son, the son fell into the vat, he bobbed on the top of the molten steel and begged his father to push him under with a rod, which his father did, this made me feel much better, not! Those huge ingots stood like monoliths in memory to the dead, they were never used, just left in an area at the rear of the factory, the men who worked there called it the graveyard and, believe me, there were quite a few ingots and it was a very big graveyard, they also had a building they called the Black Museum with objects of near-death escapes, such as protective glasses with spikes sticking out of them, helmets cut in half and spattered with molten metal, skin and blood, this was a dangerous job but good money and regular so I took it. The first job they gave me to do was a repair on what they called the 'wicket', the wicket was a door to one of the many furnaces, trouble was it was white hot, how they even got within ten feet without being severely burned puzzled me, but on occasion it would crack with the heat and had to be repaired, the minion who was in charge said, 'look this is how to do it,' to the side of the glowing door was what appeared to be a forty-five gallon steel drum full of water, he picked up his trowel and a pan of sponella, which was a crushed brick paste used to stick the bricks together, walked to the side of the glowing door, thrust his spindly hands into the barrel of water and pulled out an old full-length army trench coat drenched in water, the weight of the water made the coat so heavy it seemed to buckle his legs for a second or two, after spreading the new brick with the paste he proceeded to fling the dripping wet coat over his head and shoulders he walked crouching hooded like death stalking his prey, defending his eyes from the searing heat with his hands as he neared the glowing white-hot furnace door to replace the missing brick, within ten seconds the coat started to smoulder and after fifteen seconds it burst into flame to be thrown back into the barrel of water, 'job done,' he said, dumbstruck I was looking around for Jeremy Beadle, 'nah,' thinking to myself, 'this is a wind up.' 'Okay,' he said, 'off to the next job.' What! The next job was the soaking pits, 'you are allowed two pints of beer for the next job,' he said, and proceeded to offer me two beer tickets, tempting me towards the bar at the end of the furnace just behind the wagons, inviting me to drink the thirst-quenching liquid that would more than likely send my mind tumbling into turmoil and into the molten vats of steel should I succumb, but I declined. The soaking pits were about six meters long by four meters wide and about three meters deep, there were about twenty of them in a row and they were used to hold the white-hot ingots which were transported there by an overhead crane, the walls of the pits often got damaged with the huge steels hitting the firebrick sides, trouble was, they only let the pits cool for a day, even then they glowed red and looked like how many artists portrayed the entrance to the Christian hell, the ladder you had to climb down was steel, a wooden one would have burst into flame, then you had to repair the side wall for as long as you could stand the heat, as you descended into the glowing pit the air burned your lungs and the heat grilled your face, about two minutes was the record to stay in there and that was probably by some fire walker from the darkest jungles of Brazil, as soon as your boots touched the floor of the furnace heat was transferred through the soles, burning and stinging your feet making you dance like a cowardly cowpoke, it was as though you were walking on hot coals, 'could do with Guptah, the little Indian lad from school,' went through my mind, the only one capable of holding hot bricks whilst buttering them before laying, one minute was my limit in the pit and I was a flaming wreck, drained of energy and pouring with sweat, gasping for a pint of anything, dizzily drained and searching out the bar in the middle of the factory, no privet hedge for me, downing two pints of cool crystal-clear water in what seemed as many seconds, true, it was a real pub bar with beer pulls and glasses lining it with quite a few workers propping it up and with their free tickets to hell, they all smelt heavy from drinking, with me thinking no wonder so many people got killed, they probably were all pissed up when they fell in the vats of molten steel. Days later, walking along a line of lockers in the factory a charging arm came towards me, this was a large grab which placed scrap metal directly into the open furnaces, once the arms had discharged they would spring back at speed to refill again, so I jumped between the lockers out of its way only to be confronted by a train steaming towards me, open carriages loaded with scrap cars and such, I managed to jump out the way of that as well, at the end of the week I gave in my notice, didn't fancy spending the rest of eternity in hell or being part of a car, tank or even an ingot or some girder propping up some motorway flyover, or, come to think of it, anything that was made of metal, a few years later they closed the factory, reckon they had run out of blokes to melt down, wonder if that's where the saying 'nerves of steel' or 'an iron will' comes from? or, 'to be on your metal' or 'he was riveting'? Just kidding! Is it possible that where the body dies the spirit stays, can the human spirit be trapped for all time to eventually be taken and smelted into sheeting to be forged into other parts and pieces, those ingots that were preserved would eventually get mixed up with others to be melted down to become the ghosts in the machines, like that goddamned car that won't start, or that telly that blinkers, you know the odd strange things that happen in times of stress, maybe the spirits of the dead can be trapped and encased, destined to haunt for all time not knowing they are dead and part of the unexplained.

Martin was born on the 1st December 1971, sitting in the holding room they would not let you in for the birth in those days, it was too gruesome for a feeble man to stand, most blokes nowadays are made to watch the birth as a kind of penance for their lust and an excuse for the wife to gouge pieces out of them in retribution, Elsie would say about sex, 'a moment of pleasure and a lifetime of misery', could say the same about the temptation of the free tickets from that fellow who lives amongst the flames, 'a lifetime of pleasure and an eternity of misery'. Sitting in the room at the end of the ward, oddly there were quite a few women screaming but I could tell Jean's screams and, boy, did I feel guilty. 'What have you done?' went through my mind, Jean gave birth about nine o'clock at night, for me to be sent home sweating, weak and a nervous wreck, completely exhausted, the next day, upon entering the ward and seeing Jean, what a relief, she was still alive with the baby in her arms, my first words were, 'God he's ugly', he looked like Plug from the *Beano* that's probably where the saying 'Plug Ugly' comes from, on each side of his head was a red mark where they had used the forceps to pull him out, on closer inspection that's all they were you never know they might have been horns, and was I glad I was never tempted by that beer ticket to hell, the days passed and we left hospital, Jean's stitches were killing her and she was walking like John Wayne. The nurse said to me, 'have you got any food in?' 'Oh yes there's a nice joint of beef in the oven, roasted tatties 'n gravy,' I replied in my Wurzel voice, Jean burst out laughing, the nurse emphasized *'for the baby'* with a grim look on her face. After a few months we managed to get a council flat in a multi-story block due to the fact that our wages were poor, we were in lodgings so we qualified under the council points system because we had a young son, we were grateful for it at the time although it was depressing, but in those early days of high-rise people did make the effort to keep them clean because they were occupied by working families unlike nowadays, Martin had lost his plug-ugly looks and turned out to be a pretty and happy lad who laughed all the time at the stories Jeff had narrated to me as a child, after a while we were offered a house which we accepted knowing there was a garden for Martin to play in, and also it was near Jean's mom's and, being retired, she was prepared to look after Martin which meant we could both be working again.

It was round about this time that I realised something was going on in my head, Jean turned up from work with a small seal-point Siamese cat that she had rescued, I took to him, adopted him, fed him and got to love his ways of greeting me when returning home from a day's graft, we had a neighbour who hated cats and all things to do with life, one day he kicked my pal and was warned of the pending doom from my fist, two weeks later my little friend went out never to return again, after searching for hours I found his pure white form, black and twisted lying in a gutter by the roadside two miles away, he must have been carried off and dumped, he never went that far never even left the house only on rare occasions, looking out the window at the suspect and in anger muttering to myself 'if he is responsible for those actions' silently cursing him with a vile death, six months later he was dead, not only that, a couple of weeks after his death his wife also died the same death, Jean nonchalantly said, 'you must have put a curse on them.' I shrugged and said, 'don't blame me, they were just muttered words of anger, it's just coincidence'. Now, thinking back, can we curse people? We can think in our minds and from that we can create beauty, why can't we curse in our minds and create great destruction? But if ever I did do any harm to anyone I did not do it knowingly. There were to many times when such things occurred to be a coincidence, but then really odd things started to happen to me, people who knew me would stop me and say what were you doing in such a shop in the town, they said they had spoken to me in those places although I had not been physically there, and I had been seen on many occasions doing unusual things, with me thinking, 'how strange, what was going on?' A change was about to enter my life, a drastic change, reaching twenty-seven years of age I started to develop a desire to look at the stars, a sort of obsession came over me, I started to read star maps, charts and books: was God an astronaut? landing pads in Peru and anything about aliens, and then I decided to build an optical instrument, don't ask me why, knowing nothing about optics except those in a pub, but I needed to know what was going on. The more the reading, the bigger the obsession grew. Lenses, had to find lenses, I stripped out old microscopes and anything optical, found a concave mirror from an old Newtonian telescope Ron had owned many years before and started to read books about parabolas, hyperbolas and dissection of cones designed to bend light to a focal point, there was a pattern in my head and it was trying to configure the lenses to that pattern and to my dreams, sometimes I awoke abruptly from my sleep with messages in my head: 'the library, join the library,' the voices in my head would say, 'optical books, learn, you must learn.' In the daytime all my spare minutes were spent at the library researching books, at night my mind and face always turned to the stars, endless nights of just gazing, it became an obsession, often there were strange objects in the sky and time seemed to pass too quickly, I walked out to the shops one night and, glaring upwards, wondering at the heavens, three bright lights appeared hovering and circling above my head, the hair on the back of my neck tingled with excitement, fear and static energy, the couple who walked in front of me had not noticed, I wanted to shout 'look, look', but was afraid they would see nothing and declined, the lights shot upwards into the sky, three points of light forming a triangle to reach an altitude where they melted amongst the stars and then divided and separated, all three lights shooting off in a different directions, I dashed back to the flat excitedly and explained it all to Jean who looked at me with a kind of pity on her face and a look that said, 'you're not where it's at'. It was just after that close encounter that the lens configuration came to fruition, I locked myself away from mankind every night for weeks configuring the lenses and the mirror, becoming scruffy, unshaven and unwashed, convinced of my own insanity if my ideas did not work out, then, at last, there before me lay my creation, mirror at one end, the other packed with the lens configuration, I lifted it tentatively, holding it to my shoulder as a soldier would a bazooka and peered through it for the first time, into the heavens towards the moon, the magnification was so great that one slight movement and the moon shot past the field of view at high speed, stepping back in awe of, I skimmed the surface of the moon, never having seen such a sight, flying over the craters, in my mind machine there were no horizons, just miles and miles of craters and mountains, beyond were the satellites of Mars and the rings of Saturn, and the scary thing was - it was a familiar place and I knew the way. 'Jean, Jean, look through this lens.' She was amazed, this changed me, convinced me, a driving power came from within me, I needed to make contact, I was out most nights glaring up at the sky, watching and waiting and asking myself, 'is this my time? Is this why I feel strange on this hostile world? Am I going home at last?' Seeing many strange lights and feeling strange, the sunlight became my enemy, I avoided it as much as possible and people were starting to irritate me. 'What's the matter with them they all seem possessed?' They would talk to me but the voices were just buzzing noises in the background, Jean would stop and chat to people in the street whilst walking Martin who was in the pram, but all that was on my mind was my obsession, I felt uneasy amongst these creatures, nothing they said made sense, was I going the same path as Ron, spiralling towards a nervous breakdown, was the trauma of my past catching up with me? 'Is this how you turn mad? It was possible to look

Pete Davies

at people as they passed me by and know the doomed ones, they had this aura of death or life about them, it was easy to distinguish all people's problems with my second sight and have power over them, to curse them and turn them into dust, even to foretell events before they happened, was this what Elsie meant when she sat me on her lap that night long, long ago. 'Help me, Mom, please help me, stop me loosing myself in this strange world,' I prayed. The following night, three triangular shapes similar in shape to stealth fighters crossed through the heavens, a heavenly glow surrounding them, they flew in a formation, one up front, two behind, forming a larger triangle, a star came out of each craft and descended down from the heavens, they hovered in a triangle above my head and then descended *within* me, 'Jean, Jean,' I shouted frantically, 'come outside quick, look, look'. Pointing towards the night sky. 'Is this it? Please, please see them,' 'Oh my god,' she replied as we both gazed into the heavens, it was that moment, reaching the crossroads in my mind, the tears welled down my face in the darkness of my night and my mind opened up to the brightness of my coming day for I knew I was sane, as sane at least as others, suddenly the boiling pot that was my mind reduced to a simmer and has been simmering ever since. As for the mind machine it has been dismantled. Was it the door, the gateway to insanity? Was it looking in on me? Was it built by my hand as a tool, a window, to look into another world, to look into another dimension, into that strange world which frightened me into a realization which at that moment in time I was not ready for? Having entered through the door, at that point there would have been no way to get back homeward, but where is my home? Now that door is closed although I can't find the key in my head to lock it out forever and, though that line is cut, it is not quite the end, so it's goodbye for now till it opens again, and before I do open it, I will learn to control the wonders that lie behind because from that experience I have now become a seeker.

The machines turned and the iron ore flowed as we progressed through the seventies, but in our communities there was unrest amongst us working classes, strikes upon strikes, the unions dominating the state of play with policies which most of us did not agree with, music had lost its way, pop stars dressed like Max Wall and were ten times more promiscuous, prancing around in spandex, grown men wearing makeup like clowns, music had died and been resurrected as muzak, the children of the revolution, flower power and the created race were running amok, daring to have a voice, the country was on its knees through bad management orchestrated by the likes of Ted Heath, who played his piano whilst the ship went down, and the lights went out all over Britain, the unions, formed by the people for the people, were imploding, what we needed was a William Wilberforce to represent us but all we had was an Arthur Scargil and a red Robbo and they had not the education of the upper classes, fighting for our jobs was a lost cause, politicians came and went and failed this country and its people, the factory gates were shut, the vats empty and the furnaces cold, the red iron ceased to pour, we were told that our coal was not worth digging and our steel was not worth making, it was deemed we were all worthless and so we were scrapped by our own government, they bought cheaper, imported products because that government and all the other preceding governments never put back what they took out, never invested in British industry and British workmanship, they never even supplied so much as a damp army coat at British steel, 'British steel' now there are two words to be proud of, men and women made of British steel just bled till they became obsolete and out of date, sold out to the likes of Germany and Japan who could surpass us with production and cheapness because they had invested and modernized since the war, they weighed the scrap in from the battle fields and got rich whilst we, Britain, spent the next fifty years paying off our debts, but we, the lower working classes, were the spine of this great nation and that spine was ripped out without mercy by the closing of our factories, docks and pits, thus ending our social life and community spirit, at that time you could feel and see the fear in the eyes and on the faces in our working class communities, grown men like small children thrown out onto the street for the first time, lost and bewildered, not knowing what to do without work though paid for with a pittance, missed by those who knew no better than to march up and down with placards in protest only to be beaten into submission by the blue army. But in my eyes what really happened was that we were released from the chains of poverty, allowed to buy decent homes, freed from damp filthy conditions of deprivation and respiratory diseases, from the evils which our ancestors had lived with, inherited and worked with for generations. You can't break the British people's spirit. We let the thoughtless politicians carry on, these so-called governments get on our nerves, waste our money and lie to us but they seem to forget that walking amongst us working classes are great soldiers and thinking minds and one day the politicians may go too far with their wastage and lying. But also, with change, people change and, sadly, it goes to a higher level, we workers stand proud and still have our working-class roots, unlike the nouveaux-middle classes who have working-class roots but frown upon the places they were born. Hiding their own accents and their dress, they try to dissemble their past of which they are ashamed for fear that the middle classes whom they mix with and admire will discover that they are just peasants in disguise - which they are, betraying their generation. If ever you should have the misfortune to meet me, the first thing you will notice is my black country accent, broad and plain for all to hear, because this is me, never hiding the roots of my past for fear of, say, not getting that job or not impressing that fool or not mixing with that class, proud of my birthright which is from a generation that was born to graft, to speak the truth, to be true to oneself and to be honest, these were the basic fundamentals we learned as kids at an early age, not to lie, cheat, confuse and omit truth for personal gain, surely this is the foundation that all great countries and governments are built on?

By 1982, Elvis was dead, John Lennon was dead, and Jean's dad, Harry, was about to die, he went to work on the morning and never came back home, Jean's mom phoned us at eight o'clock in the evening worried that he had not come back from work, it was getting dark so we went to the small factory where he worked, it was closed, after searching the streets we eventually found him slumped in a bus shelter, he was a diabetic, he had had a stroke and had lain there for six hours with people stepping over his body to catch the bus, we got him to hospital but, sadly, he died the day after, aged sixty-four and just about to retire. Jean's mom and dad had often spoke and planned for what they would do in retirement and they were looking forward to the rest. According to the shop keeper by the bus stop, Harry was slurring when he asked for help and they thought he was a drunk, so they just left him there to die, even the Salvation-Army bloke who stood in the queue ignored him, such is the way the world has become, we are all running scared, a phone call to the police or emergency services might have saved his life. Harry was an avid bird lover and bred budgies for years, the night he died Jean and her mother lit a candle in the window for him and his spirit, it was their way of

saying goodbye, the next day getting up before the others and on the window sill where the candle had burned was a small pile of wax and before me was the perfect shape of a bird, wings and all, the wax had melted to form the shape of the bird and the wax run from the candle had formed a perch which the bird sat on, Jean said to me she would never had noticed had it not been pointed it out to her, this wax bird gave

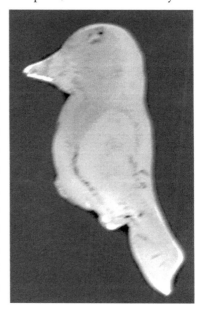

her mother and her some kind of solace and contentment, but when she showed it the vicar who conducted the funeral, he just patted her on the hand and said, 'yes dear', he might as well have said, 'how long have you believed in fairies?' There are many spirit messages like this but we miss them due to grief at the time of being exposed to them, look and you will find, there is likely a spirit message from a loved one telling you all is well and a last goodbye, When Jean and I visited Swadlincote village fair, at Christmas 2012, the town was buzzing with people hence the reason I took my camera, walking down one of the back streets away from the noise we came upon a church-door entrance, we were kind of drawn to it and decided to go in and that was strange in itself because we find churches quite boring, inside we found an appeal had been organized and it was to aid the starving children of this world, as we read on I could see the tears forming in Jean's eyes and she donated an amount of money, a few minutes before leaving I decided to take this picture of Jean purchasing a candle because of the colourfulness of the

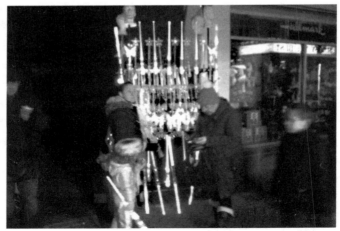

event, if you look to the right hand corner of the photo there is an undisputable ghostly figure of a child praying reflected in the window of the closed shop, I know, some sceptics will say it is a reflection, but first of all, if it is, surely it would be lower to the ground? And ask yourselves, what would what seems to be a naked child be doing praying on a cold winters night? It's odd but normally I never blow up pictures on the computor but for some reason I felt obliged to in this case and so revealed this spiritual message of gratitude. You have to look for the signs, remember the day my spastic sister passed away and told my mother there was a man in the sky waiting and beckoning her on as she was passing away? She knew nothing of religion or gods or death but somehow the puzzle of life had raised its head, so don't discount any possibilities, my brother Ron has his opinions and so does every other religion and surely each of you will also reach your final destiny in your minds. In life all downsides have an upside, a few months later Jean's mother received an insurance payment from the death of Harry and she gave all her kids, Cedric, Keith and Jean, one thousand pounds each, she said she wanted them to have it whilst she was able to see them enjoy it, Jean took up Margaret Thatcher's offer and the money gave us a deposit and a chance to buy our council house which we did.

Never in my life have I been a defeatist and nothing will ever deter me from truth or justice, on one occasion when Martin, my young son, had reached eleven years of age, the film *E.T.* about the extra-terrestrial came out, Martin was obsessed with bikes having at that time one of those early chopper bikes, the ones with the large saddles, very nostalgic now but sadly gone, the fad at that time was for B.M.X. born from *E.T.*, Martin continually asked me for a new bike for the coming Christmas and he wanted a B.M.X. so, as you do, we looked around and found a new import in a local shop, the bike was a Kuwarah, made in Japan, it was a revelation because it was the first of its kind in the U.K. other than in the *E.T.* film, it was very individual because it had a distinguishing red frame with white-walled tyres and the rising sun motif on the tyres and the frame, we went out on a limb and purchased it on weekly payments at the cost of £150, he loved it, he travelled everywhere with his friends, mimicking the antics of B.M.X., he had the bike for about a week then one day he never came home at his specified time and it started to go dark, you can imagine our panic, we searched everywhere, eventually we found him alone in a large park not far from the house where we lived, crying, cold and frightened, were we relieved, he had been out with his friends with his bike near the Scotland's, the ugly place from my childhood, yes, the same place, he had been accosted by a gang of bullies who took his bike off him so he had to make his way back home alone, on foot and about four miles from the robbery, had we known he would end up in that area any time in his life he would have been warned of the dangers, but because we lived miles away it never occurred to me to mention it. The next day we paid a visit to the police station, Martin gave a good description of the thief but we were told of the improbability of finding the culprit or the bike, knowing these bullies, their habitation and their style, if you can call it that, these were probably the next generation of the ones who used to bully me when a young kid, vulnerable and unable to defend myself against the groups of cowardly losers. From that day on I made it my business to pursue those losers, every night, after coming home from work and finishing my tea, all my evenings were spent trawling the streets and haunts where they lived and assembled, after a week or so of searching, I came across a gang of teenagers messing about in a pub car park, the thing that hit me straight in the eye was that one of them had a B.M.X. bike with a white-walled tyre with a rising sun motif, got ya, I stopped the car and waded into the pack of losers to grab hold of the kid with the bike and asked him, 'where did you get that tyre from?' The gang tried to intimidate me by pushing me from the back but they were only kids about fourteen to sixteen years of age, they stood no chance against a thirty-one-year-old who was as fit as a fiddle, tempered by the building trade, those bullies did not intimidate me, call it the David and Goliath factor, but the true logical version is that Goliath will paste David every time, stone or no stone. 'Where did you get it from?' The kid would not say so, grabbing him by the scruff off the neck, I frog-marched him and his bike to his house, his parents genuinely seemed shocked about the incident, I told them, if their son did not say where he got the parts the police would be involved, the kid blurted out, 'Jason, Jason gave it to me,' and he then gave me Jason's address, I had the wisdom not to confront the thief single-handed because thieves are bred by thieves and they are cleverer and smarter than most people give them credit for, most arrests come from thieves who grass on their own not from the intelligence of the police force, which is why the police are always on telly asking for information, tantalizing grasses with amounts of money they will never get, they say you have to set a thief to catch a thief which really means, 'know your adversary', and I had the advantage of knowing my adversaries well throughout the years of running the gauntlet amongst them. With the law on my side, we visited the house of the thief, we sat in the police car, Jean, Martin and me, the officer got out, proceeded up the path and knocked on the door and the thief appeared at the door, he was dressed exactly as Martin had described him the day he stole the bike and he fitted the description Martin gave the police to a tee, except he had his hair cut which was long at the time of the robbery. 'That's him, Dad,' Martin said to me with tears in his eyes, we sat in the police car outside the house and the officer spent about five minutes at the door questioning the occupants, he came back to the car. 'It's not him,' he said, 'he's got short hair.' Martin said, 'it is him, look he is wearing the clothes exactly as described.' 'We can't go prosecuting people on that evidence,' the officer said, 'so let that be an end to it.' After several months of harassing, the police finally they agreed to search the property, to find that this person was a fostered child and he had built a small business stealing and stripping bikes to order together with his guardian, the many parts the police found at the property were packed professionally and made ready for re-sale, the case went to court and the sentence was to repay us ten pounds at fifty pence per week, when the thief and the social worker left the court they were happy and smiling at the result, needless to say we never got any compensation, not even the insulting fifty pence per week, we were called to the police station a week or so later to collect the remains of the bike found at the house, it consisted of one chain and one tyre and we still had to pay the remaining instalments for the bike, we don't hold a grudge because that thief would only go on to do greater crimes encouraged by the verdict of the jury and the wisdom of the judge, the same with the social worker but that did not matter to me, it is the other judge they have to worry about, Elsie's judge and my judge, the invisible judge, the final judge, from which there is no escape, for justice will hunt them down, whether it be in this life or the next he will come for them in their darkest hour and their darkest night, and if justice does not prevail or he feels cheated by death he will search the next generation and generations to come till he can hand out that justice, eventually to catch up with all thieves, liars, cheats and killers.

Occasionally I have met what is termed as 'Aliens here on Earth' undesirable or not, when starting my own building-maintenance company, doing contract work for Birmingham Council, we were called out on emergencies and close encounters of the odd kind and boldly went where no man had gone before - or would want to. As an avid reader of sci-fi and as a kid, I remember how Dan Dare had once encountered a race of beings who ate matter and anti-matter, funny enough that book came from the tip which was often rife with beings searching and looking amongst the rubbish, maybe they were some strange race searching for food or for parts for their spaceship which by some twist of fate had been stranded here, that particular area on the outskirts of the city was pretty rife with aliens, most of them wore sun glasses and only came out at night and they were very pale-skinned with eyes sunken in their heads, on one of the many occasions when I was called out to do repairs, a twenty-year-old-odd being answered the door, it was dressed in black from head to foot and its hair was bright red and trailed to its waist, upon entering the hallway everything in the flat was painted black, everything! walls, ceilings, doors, everything, sending a chill up my spine so I dropped back to let it lead the way, the rooms were piled high with rotting bags of dustbin waste with the contents spewing everywhere creating a foul smell as the flies blackened the air, I was constantly on my guard whilst fixing the problem, often looking over my shoulder, after finishing the job and asking to wash my hands it led me to a toilet room, the strange thing was, although the house was filthy, the walls of the toilet had brand new shelving all around, and on those shelves must have been two hundred or more bottles of unopened ordinary bleach, whilst washing my hands in the corner of the room, I noticed the toilet was draped with what seemed like thick red hair, it touched the floor, went over the rim, down the pan and submerged in the water, none of the white porcelain was visible, the thing had left the room and by this time and I was having visions of it metamorphosing and scuffling back into the toilet with tentacles flaying and a massive grotesque head about to devour me, hacking and chopping at me with its octopus-shaped beak, therefore I made my exit as quickly as possible, the only explanation is that the being must have been hooked on some sort of bleach gas like a Martian chlorine gas guzzler, the Type-Three version in my Dan-Dare catalogue of weirdo's, hence the hair to the toilet, the only way the hair could have got there was it must have put its head deep into the toilet pan to inhale the bleach gas, and it must have done that several thousand times to completely cover the porcelain, or, was it a wig, which it used to disguise itself in its human form when it went to the supermarket skip or the tip, rummaging for food? There are many stories like this from my contracting days, like the thirty-year-old woman who did not know how to flush the constantly overflowing faeces filled toilet and never had till I learned her, or the strange family who kept used toilet paper and nappies packed sky high in every cupboard of the house, or the man who complained of the damp patch to the floor of his living room which was half full of used tea bags, how strange you humans are. Now, it is a big universe out there and, after seeing many strange things and meeting many strange people and trying to work out logically the reasons for their actions, I have come to the conclusion that aliens do exist. After all what do we term as an 'alien'? To me, it's something that exists but does not have the mannerisms of a human, how can the human race be so naïve as to think they are the only ones in the vastness of time and space? most people will tell you they have seen strange happenings and events in the sky, things they can't explain, but they are frowned upon by others who have not encountered anything or who have encountered something but wish to keep the secret in order to avoid ridicule. Recently, passing the area where the red-haired being lived, which I am not at liberty to divulge, the habitats had gone leaving a waste land behind, the question in my mind is, who removed them? Or did they one stormy night decide to leave this planet, leaving a gaping hole where their spaceship once sat? Come to think of it, my brain refuses to think like a human in many ways, maybe my mind was ejected from one of those Roswell spacecraft just before it crash landed in the desert in America after arriving at the same time here on earth, in 1947, there are bound to be more aliens like me, some probably born the same year and trying to contact each other through some greater power and all of us thinking the same about the human race: 'why has he done that?' 'why does she do that?' 'why do they think like that?' 'why are they so stupid? 'why are they so greedy?' Maybe my existence has been taken over by that greater force or power, sometimes we read of Christianity and Christian beliefs of the creation of the world in six days and of the seventh day when even their lord rested, and whilst he rested the seventh day was born, bringing rest, peace and contentment, hence the reoccurring seven. You may call me an agnostic or a blasphemer, bet you don't call believers of other religions blasphemers, all religions have a point and, let's face it, when a new idea comes along most of you will ridicule it through sheer fear of not understanding or through fear of retribution from your god for even considering it, someone once asked me to take part in a ouija-board session when very young, the other kids thought I was stupid and scared for refusing to take part but, even at that age, I knew not to play with the unknown, not to open one of those many secret doors in my mind, it's the brain that becomes confused when you mess with things like that, and when people are involved they can manipulate movement as they always do on this planet confusing reality - why do you think that no miracle-workers have ever come forward to claim the endless millions of pounds' worth of prizes offered by researchers on the internet for anyone who is genuine, to be tested under controlled conditions? The James Randi Educational Foundation, for one, are offering untold wealth, but, there again, if you had those powers you would not need the likes of the James Randi Educational Foundation would you? It reminds me of when John Lennon was once, allegedly, asked by the Maharishi why he was leaving the ashram, 'if you're so cosmic you will know the answer,' was John's reply. To a weak-minded person the occult can become a reality which can be twisted out of shape and out of that twisting is born confusion and why confuse myself? My beliefs are for me, a set of ideas which make me happy and explain to me why the world is like it is, and I am fortunate enough to be able to speak for the benefit of others who want me to.

Unfortunately for me, this world of yours is full of strange dimensions and odd events, by the mid-Nineties I was doing a lot of work on army camps most of it was in isolated areas - moors, plains and such, miles from civilization - one afternoon, whilst taking a break beside a forest glade, the tranquillity of the place and heat of the sun encouraged me to drift into a deep sleep, dreaming of walking through a wood and surrounded by tall pine trees, a while later I awoke to find the afternoon had passed so I headed for home, upon arriving in our street a pack of dogs started barking at me excessively, which was unusual having never noticed them in the street before, then overnight I developed a pain to my right hand, a kind of tingling stinging, and it was starting to blacken, by the next morning what seemed to be a bloody bite-mark had appeared between my thumb and forefinger, the punctures were two inches apart and they were deep, the bite-mark was surrounded by a redness and caused a blackening to my hand, I showed Jean and all she did was burst out laughing, probably thought how childish of me for moaning about it, as the day passed the pain receded but for two weeks the marks remained, two weeks after that I was feeling dizzy at work and starting to see a red twinkling sky with black stars and also there were rushing noises in my head, my strength left me, I grew weaker and weaker, I curled up in a foetal position in a lone field miles from nowhere, needing to get home, I just about made it through the psychedelic kaleidoscope of traffic, the signs to the roads and footpaths bowing and bending as though I was passing through a cyclone, arriving at my doorstep my eyes began to fade, for me to stagger through the doorway and collapse on the settee in our living room and lay there, weak and disorientated, for what seemed hours, after a while a large

Pete Davies

black wolf materialised to lay himself by my side and comfort me, putting my arm around him we just lay there absorbing each other's warmth. I was floating and drifting in and out of consciousness for the next three days, paralysed in confusion and confronted by many demons and predators that fancied their chances of conscripting me into their dark ranks, and, whilst lying there, the Demon Lord appeared before me, sat beside me, said he knew of me well, befriending me, he spoke of his plans to rule this world, told me that there was a place for my kind amongst his pack and there would be great rewards and to join him in this war which he seemed to think he was winning, I knew that if he could not convince me he would try to seduce me and, if he could not seduce me into his realm, he would try to silence me for good, as I am sure he has on many occasions, and, once succumbed, I knew I would be lost forever, so I faced the cause of all death and destruction, who was here on this earth before we came, and declined his attractive offer of wealth, health and power, and in his rage he sent more visions of horror and despair to drive me insane, but what is sanity? My mind and my dark companion stood firm against the plague of creatures bent on devouring me into the pits of their stomachs and into the belly of the beast, but, you see, like you all, from within I have my own demon, and with glaring diamond eyes and bared chrome teeth I defended myself and it kept me from harm, and, when Jean appeared to check on me, the demon would hide within me as though we were one. At that time there was an epidemic of meningitis going around and that was a constant worry to Jean, but that wolf constantly lay by my side, and we stood together against the onslaught of demons which attacked for those three days and nights, and when the dark died, our eyes awaiting to meet each dawn, my companion never left my side, and on the third day he started to lick my face and my silence was shattered by the wailing sound inside my head and the wolf's saliva was like beads of sweat running down my back and face, my body was throbbing with pain. My three self-imposed days of quarantine were up. I staggered to the bathroom and, running the tap, drank what seemed like gallons of water to satisfy my thirst and to quench the fire burning in my soul, I climbed into the bath and the splashing of the water awoke Jean who was sleeping in the bed that I had not seen for three days and three nights, 'oh, you're feeling better,' she shouted, imagining I was having a bath, 'ring for an ambulance,' was my reply, screaming, 'my body's burning.' She came running into the bathroom and stared into the vacuum of my eyes which were black and sunken into my hirsute, gaunt and drawn face, she rushed downstairs, '999 please', the medics arrived and checked me over, 'can't see anything wrong,' they said. 'There's meningitis about, maybe he has it,' said Jean and they looked and thought for a moment. 'Okay, we'll take him for a check-over.' Regaining consciousness in a hospital bed, wired and dripped, quarantined and isolated, the doctors asked me questions, 'have you been abroad recently?' 'Have you had contact with any wild animals?' My lungs were collapsing, 'rabies, or malaria?' the doctor quizzed, 'seems like rabies.' hearing through the haze of my mind. This went on for five days finally to be taken out of isolation with me feeling better, signing myself out from the ward much to Jean's displeasure, the reason was that they had mixed me with the dying and there was no way I was about to die and leave this world, there's much to do. Weeks past and I got better, I felt strong and ready to go back to work, then a burning pain came to my spine and travelled down my legs, causing me agony, and, from that day for twenty years, I suffered those burning pains at least once, sometimes twice, a month, it was that same pain I suffered in France when I lay for seventeen days in agony and was told by the doctors that it was gout, but they never gave me a cure, the constant pain one day would be the same again tomorrow and that pain often came in the night and was severe, it mostly seemed to be at times of the full silvery moon, to leave me writhing with agony for several days after, the only cure was to continue to drink gallons and gallons of water, flushing my system during the times of agony, suffering those agonies from that time till January 2011 when, visiting another English doctor upon returning to England, he did some tests on me and said there was nothing wrong, my blood was clear of any contamination of uric acids and told me to come back in six months, but I was in agony again, my joints were swelling up double the size and crippling me, no way was a fool going to tell me there was nothing wrong when I was in pain, the following night lying awake in agony, repetitious of the many times over the many years, meditating back to my vagabond years when a child locked away in that lonely place when hungry and it was Tommy's word, I spoke to my creator about the bond we have, enclosed and cleared my mind and drew the power and energy that surrounds us all, and the power entered my body. We all can do this, you don't need crystals, bones or writings on walls, we all have this power and energy within us, on the right hand is the positive, on the left is the negative, slowly join the positive to the negative and you will open the gateway and have the answer to all suffering – and, as a backup, the next day hobbling along to A&E, eventually to be seen by a lady doctor, 'I know what's wrong with you,' she said, 'take this.' and within one hour the pain was gone, within four hours the swelling had gone. Who was that woman that could cure something after so many years those others could not? to me she was my angel, still have my great fear of water but have not bayed the moon in agony since and have also got rid of that damned silver bangle found at the tip as a kid - and thanked my Doberman for laying with me through those three dark days and nights, mentally promising her when her time is near or in her times of need she could rely on me too.

Many people who know me ask me to wish wealth and good fortune upon them, they seem to think that money always goes to those who don't deserve it, but maybe it goes to those who deserve the curse of it, to me money is a curse, so why curse them with wealth when wealth is not the key? And what a deadly weapon it can be in the wrong hands, most don't know what to do with their new-found wealth, some purchase a new house, cars and a boat then speak of the misery it brings on them, they can't see the opportunity they have been given by fate to do something good, there are always deserving causes desperate for them to donate money to them to help the less fortunate, maybe a win is a test given by fate or an opportunity to make someone happy, the thing with life is it's the chase, the struggle to get what one wants and desires, once you have met those desires they fade to nothing and you will be lost, but the desire to own attracts undesirables with the same desires who cannot own through one misfortune or another, that desire to own leads to greed, jealousy and hate, these are the fortunes that money brings, humans want to know the worth of everything that is owned and they dribble with greed when told that the value of their possession is high and are downcast when told that it is low, crying and snivelling. It really doesn't matter if you are poor or wealthy, if you are wealthy you may take that cruise or yachting trip but fate always has a way of messing it up one way or another, and if you are poor you can still live life to the full because money can only buy inanimate objects which after a short time will be ditched for the next fad. Don't yearn to gain large amounts of money through some twist of fate because for every positive there is a negative, and for everything you gain in this life I can guarantee you will lose something very precious, balance is the key.

By 1990, the council contract had ended, we sold the council house and moved, it was not an affluent area, the new property was small, detached, pretty run down and cheap with a shared drive, an elderly man lived at the back whom we never saw too often. After winning a contract with a large building company, they offered me a sub-contract working in an establishment that was for their eyes only if you get the gist, and there were quite a few eye openers, I nearly lost my life again but my angel always steps in, but there was one particular event that stays in my mind, I was asked to repair a cracked water main, according to my minder it was in an experimental laboratory in which particular experiments had been going for eight years. Upon entering the top-security establishment I noticed large glass tubes with some sort of beings floating in a transparent fluid, and there were quite a few of them, Aliens, is the only way to describe them, they were wired with all sorts of electronics and such, twitching spasmodically in their individual floating prisons, the glass tubes each stood six to seven feet high with a circumference of about six feet, thus giving me an idea of perspective, the creatures were about four foot tall with spindly arms and legs, they looked as though the skin had been peeled from their bodies, it was as though they had suffered third degree burns to the whole of their torsos, but that's my opinion, and one of Mom's philosophies in life was, 'believe nothing of what you hear and only half of what you see,' and I have always stuck to that. To be convinced they were aliens I would have to talk to them or see them walking around with ray guns zapping us all, so you see I have to combine solid evidence before I comment, but I do speak to strange beings in my subconscious, messages sometimes enter my head as though guiding me to the right path, Jean often complains of me speaking to the devil in my sleep and it is in some sort of language of tongues that only him and I understand, but am I communicating with him, or is it the others, them, the shades, the greys as they are named? Or are they communicating with me? I have seen many pictures of aliens, as drawn by U.F.O. abductees and I suggest those poor individuals were very similar, and to my mind when I think back, they were pretty similar to that thing that crossed the window those many years before when Dianne brought one of the Devil's disciples to stay - and were they imps Mom spoke of at my birth, or aliens? My mind tells me that all these mysteries, such as aliens, demons, humans, devils, angels and gods are entwined one way or another. My guard watched over me while I carried out certain work within the area, and the reason he watched over me was because I had not passed a security test tracing back generations of my family, there just weren't any! Anyway the job was to turn off a water service to the particular building that housed the experiment and to renew the water main which had corroded, after arranging for all disastrous contingencies, I brought in a mini digger and we started to excavate the damaged water service, digging down about twelve feet below ground level, then we finished the excavation by climbing down a ladder into the trench and excavating the remainder of the six-inch water pipe by hand. I had just cut through the damaged area with a steel saw to allow me to renew the fracture with the new part, when, just at that moment, one of the guards came running towards the secured site, 'stop! stop!' he hollers, 'I've turned the wrong service off,' and with a large key he turns on the water hydrant without any regard for me trapped in the twelve-foot-deep trench with no way out, there again I was expendable to those thoughtless - what should I call them - humans? The pipe I was cutting exploded, blowing the steel bush into the air and the water gushed like an oil well with me in the hole, water is not my forte and the trench filled with a tremendous speed, luckily for me there was an electrical duct six feet below the ground running parallel with the trench, the huge piece of steel whizzed past my forehead scraping a piece of skin off as it passed and penetrated the concrete cover of the electrical duct allowing the water to drain away and for me to survive once more to tell of this story. Often the employees of that establishment would show me an incoming U.F.O. on the radar tracking system, it was a standard normal occurrence to them, one guard told me, 'it comes down from outer space at twelve every day and stays in the same place showing as a stationary blip on the radar screen, we have sent fighters to see what it is but as soon as they are within any reasonable distance it just disappears off the radar back into space again,' and they were so casual about it because it was an everyday occurrence. Now I once read a book called *Kink* and it was written by Dave Davies, my reading was inspired by a documentary I once watched about him and to which I felt an immediate connection, I would not say spiritual, it was as though he was an old friend from some other life somewhere in the universe, it's hard to explain because I haven't quite understood all the pieces yet, that book was the inspiration that led me to write this piece, maybe *Kink* is a beacon, a signal or a message to people like me, seekers searching for the right code to bring our minds into action, to join minds together, not only Dave Davies, there are bound to be many others, thinking and doing the same things, since I read that book it is like I have found another piece of the code of life and death and understand a lot more, *but* - and it's quite a big but - minds can be twisted out of shape by other interferences to lead one on the wrong track, interferences such as humanoids, weirdoes, creeps and hangers-on who will say and do anything for their fifteen minutes, especially where fame and fortune are involved which is why I mention it. Dave Davies experienced a great revelation unto himself and, to my mind, everything he says is completely true, and according to him I bet he would love to get his hands on a 'ray gun' to sort that brother of his out, well now you know Dave - or do you? All these facts would be denied should those human gods responsible be questioned, they don't even tell the truth about the truth so why would they have a problem lying about the truth? Often they would casually show me weapons of destruction, such weird things that I never understood and at that time neither did they, I was fitting a meter in one of the seminar rooms, it was filled with foreign scientists debating and writing conclusions on a wall about some object (don't forget I am pretty good at languages, bit of German from Marlene, the French from school, Dutch from Hans, and when you know one language, especially French, it's surprising how many other languages are pretty similar), they were writing mathematical equations and such on blackboards and I asked my minder, 'what are they searching for?' 'Well,' he said, 'they've discovered a piece of technology being used here on this earth and it could be useful as a weapon of war, they have similar things but this is far more advanced, the yanks don't know where it comes from the Chinese and the Russians deny any knowledge so they are stripping it down to see what it does.' A kind of back engineering, and don't forget if those were alien body's I saw in those tubes of glass they must have come with all sorts of technology, sometimes there are programs on the television about U.FO.s but what they show you is twenty to thirty years out of date and it is so easy to confuse the masses and manipulate people, those type of institutions unite to form some sort of defensive moat, they try to ridicule you, they put   documentaries out, as conspiracy theories to divert your eyes from what they are really doing, why is it so that many people see these happenings and it all ends up being filtered to some obscure humanoid who then disappears off the face of the earth, but don't fear any of the actions or meddling by that dark warlike part of our race, to the superior power above the warlike ones are like children with a new toy but are still playing with the box, that thing hovering above them comes from a far greater civilisation and mind than theirs and it's there for a reason, watching, waiting, policing them, which is the reason I believe this earth will be here for at least another million years. You see, to me, on this planet there are two species, 'compassionate people' who have love for their fellow man, and 'humanoids', who class themselves as part of our race, who are mixed amongst us and even look like us, but are tearing us apart, I wonder how many souls have been prized from their bodies due to their actions and in the name of humanitarianism, and I can tell you all that after working in that establishment my eyes have been opened to a lot of the mysteries of life and don't be afraid because you who have love for your fellow man are not alone in this universe, and if there are those amongst you think I am making this all up: why would I, how can I? I am a seventh born and truth is my forte and part of my belief.

In 1992 came bankruptcy, this was due to many things: me not being assertive enough and not being a good business man, or even the curse of a seventh-born. Not being able or capable of getting the money owed me in quick enough, I was made bankrupt for £8,000 owed to a supplier although, at that same time, with me being owed £109,000 by various companies, sitting at the tribunal table were three persons, the liquidator, the plaintiff and me, I explained that I needed another month or two to get in some money from my debtors, I had visited the main debtor who had their head office in London and confronted them about the money they owed me several times and each time they said all would be fine, but like all big businesses they had a skill of passing the buck from office to office, a system often practiced to delay payments and, for a small contractor like me when you are alone in this world against so many, you don't stand a chance, the liquidator did not want to know although the evidence was plain to see, he made me bankrupt there and then, freezing all my assets. Why? Even to this day it bewilders me. That was one of the lowest times of my life, thirty years of hard graft down the pan for one man's decision and the wrong decision, just one more thing to add, Martin my son drove me back home from the tribunal, feeling so low and depressed, I switched on the car radio just to take my mind off things and the first song to come on was *Don't Give Up* by Willie Nelson, how appropriate, and how clever of my guardian angel. Everything was gone: vans, pride, business, our living but they never took the house because there was no equity in it - although they took my private pension to leave me with nothing for my old age, the last thing to say on the subject is that once all the other contractors and suppliers had been paid, there was £52,826 left and oddly enough that's the amount that all the administration and solicitors' bills came to, the exact amount, which left nothing, absolutely nothing, and has left me with the tainted stain of twisted justice marking my persona for the rest of my life. Jean and I sat and talked about the next move, she had done the secretarial work and invoices and had been paid out of our company and now we both had no job, no company and no money and her car had been seized so we had no transport, she took a job caring, looking after the elderly, scrubbing floors and cleaning, we desperately needed money to live, to put food in our bellies, she travelled by bus and bike from job to job till she saved £250 to buy an old banger, and then a job came up for me at a small building firm, they supplied me with a van, and then one day Jean said she had been talking to the old chap who lived at the back of us, she said he was in a right state, his clothes were ragged and dirty and his house was in such a mess, and would I go down and mend his tap so he could have a bath? She was right, the place was a tip, the old chap's house was a very small crofter's cottage with just three small rooms, totally dilapidated, how anyone could live there puzzled me, apparently at one time it had housed twelve people but that was long ago in the Dickensian era, but it was still Dickensian, there was a large hole to the roof of the bathroom and the ceiling had collapsed into the bath over the years, his only other room, in which he had his bed and cooking facilities, was filthy with no kitchen just a sink, the waste water flowed into a bucket in the middle of the room and at most times overflowed causing a foul smell, I mended the tap and arranged the hot water, he had an old, ancient electric water-heater on the wall but it was broken, after fixing it, one thing led to another, I repaired the roof, plastered the ceiling and got the bath working. 'Pete,' Jean says a few weeks later, 'you know those odd kitchen units and worktops you had left over from various jobs, could you fit them in Eric's?' So, after fitting the kitchen as ordered, he could now cook and had running water, it was wonderful to him, he was eighty-one years of age and on his own, Jean then said she was going to try to get him a grant for some work to his property - the windows and doors were as rotten as everything else - she got the grant and a few months later the contractors moved in and, lo and behold, the property was liveable, we became friends with the old chap and visited him regularly, we would sit out with him on summer nights and have a laugh and a drink and any time Jean cooked a hot dinner for us she would take him one, she did his shopping and his washing, she was already doing this as a job for other old people so it was just another job to her although unpaid. All was well, then one day Eric came to the back door of where we were living, he came in and sat on the settee and broke down in tears, we knew he liked a bet and a drink but he had spent all his money and had none left to pay his gas and electric bills, they were coming to cut him off the next day. 'Right, do you want us to take over your affairs for you?' 'Would you please,' he said. We paid his bills the next day and all was well, we sat him down at the table worked out his pension and budgeted his outgoings, it left him with about fifty pounds a week for groceries and a bet and a drink, oh, he liked a fag as well and he did the Football coupons for which he had picked the same numbers for fifty years and never won once. About a year passed and the depression of the bankruptcy was well behind us, we were okay, we were sitting one night when a knock came to the door, it was Eric and he was all dressed up, smart and clean-shaven in tie and suit. 'Can I come in?' he said. 'Certainly, you know you don't have to ask.' He sat down. 'Jean and Pete,' he said, 'having lived for eighty-four years now and in all those years have never met anyone so kind and thoughtful ...' so he had been to his solicitors that day and had instructed them to leave the property to us both when he died. Well, we stood there open-mouthed, we never knew he had no kin and we certainly never expected any gain for our deeds, we thanked him and shrugged it off and he said no more of it, then, a few months later, out of the blue, he told Jean we had an appointment with his solicitor the next day to sign the will, we had completely forgotten his promise, we traipsed across town where he was interviewed by an alternate solicitor, a precaution to safeguard the elderly against con-men, and he left us the property, at that time it still needed a lot of work doing on it there were just three very small rooms but it was a start. We carried on working into the mid-nineties when Jean's mom was taken ill. We had a spare room because Martin had got married and moved away, so we surrendered her council flat and she lived with us, and she was not on her own because Eric and her were company for each other whilst we were away at work which was most of the daylight hours. By November 1997, both Jean's mom and Eric were in hospital for what seemed to be simple problems but they both never came out and a few weeks later they died, within three weeks of each other, and we were now on our own, we renovated the property Eric had left us and we had to have a loan to pay for the materials, I worked day and night for four years on that property, even by floodlight after coming home in the dark evenings from my day job, I built a small swimming pool to the rear and an extension, on one such night when working late on the property, looking up from the trench I was working in, out of the solid wall of the house came a figure dressed in a grey jumper into the light of the floodlight, he turned and waived to me, I climbed out of the trench thinking someone was robbing the house, but there was no one, I told Jean when she came home. 'Funny that,' she said, 'on several occasions there has been someone coming up the drive or seemed to be out of the corner of my eye, and I often thought you were coming home early, anticipating your entrance to the door, to find no one there.' A few weeks later after hacking some render from a wall of the old house we exposed a doorway which had been blocked up for many years, it was our intention to open it up for use which we did and from that day never saw the apparition ever again, it would be nice to think it was a final farewell from an old friend.

Jean would come home late at night from doing her caring job which was well below minimum wage - hence the hours - and we would collapse, knackered, together, but we were happy, we moved in, we loved the house because it was totally private, and we were now back on our feet ready to face what the world could chuck at us, another year had passed and gone and we were nearing the Millennium, the area we lived in was becoming more and more run down and in the darkness the zombies began to dominate, the mindless ones who sleep all day and wait for dark to wander aimlessly around the streets awaiting their opportunity to rob and steal, when you move to inner city areas this is where every dropout seems to live, no one seemed to have, or to want a job any more, they did not want to go to work, they just wanted to rob the ones who did, we had to build a fence around our fortress and lock all the doors at night, the council in all its wisdom decided to open a half-way house two doors away from us and this created a ghetto for every loser to congregate and make their plans to rob the frail and elderly who lived in the bungalows opposite. We opposed the plans submitted by the council but we were out of our depth and we were outwitted by the council, as for the criminals, with years of experience and with the law on their side, they could walk in packs on the streets at night, dominating them whilst all decent people kept self-imposed curfews, practically every house in the street was robbed, lessons have been learned since by the police and the council but at our expense, hence the reason we purchased Spice, the Doberman, she was a good deterrent, all dogs can hear and sense a lot more than humans can, and whenever the zombies attempted to rob and steal she would lift her head and look at me and all we had to do was let her out to bark a couple of times and the thieves would scurry off into the night, they tried all sorts of tricks to injure and maim her and put her out of action, they threw broken glass over the fence to damage her paws and, in the bonfire season which lasted three months, they could purchase, detonate and propel explosives at will wherever they wanted with the law on their side, I would never live my life without a dog of some sort, even now, after the death of Spice we have this little Jack Russell and it is like having a second sense, alerting me to the dangers of zombies approaching.

Being in the building trade and always changing jobs for more money, one particular day there was an advert for maintenance workers in our local newspaper, the advert was for general building workers and it was for quite interesting work, doing various jobs, I was approaching the age of fifty and the toll of heavy work was starting to take the strain on my poor body, the wounds and injuries of the past thirty-five years were mental and physical, I had broken my leg slipping off a ladder on one occasion which left me with a slight limp, landing on the concrete floor having only fallen two feet I thought nothing of it but, when getting up, the bottom half of my leg stayed flat on the concrete and the bone came out the side of my leg, gouging through the flesh and causing it to bleed, the lad who was working with me at the time phoned for an ambulance, the thick dark blood started to run and the pain was bad followed by pulsating sledge-hammer-type blows to the area of the break, the lucky thing was, Jean had convinced me two weeks before to take out a policy to cover me for such things, Jean has always been the logical one of us and keeps us covered for accidents - my sister-in-law has a policy to buy her a coffin when she is dead, she pays thirty-five quid a month and so far she has paid in five thousand pounds, maybe she wants a state funeral, me too but paid by the state, a pauper's grave will do for me or no grave at all, don't much care to be placed back in a box, stiff as a plank and made up like Archie Andrews, the ventriloquists dummy, with rosy-red cheeks and a parting to my hair, greased down by persons who don't know me or care of me, celebrating my death with a Gottle of Geer, or even a Guinness, and I resent being told by those so-called, squeaky-clean, celebrity coffin-dodgers you see on the telly and read about in the papers telling us to buy our coffins before we die, just because we baby-boomers are getting on they think they can say and do what they want to us, bet those celebrity coffin-advisers get a free one out of it, posh and made of oak, with brass handles so that their relatives can tat them in at the scrap yard after the burning, and as a bonus a pot of best dripping after the ceremony, and a good fee for convincing us, but don't forget, you greedy thoughtless dodgers, there are no pockets in shrouds.

The slight disability from the fall was one of the reasons I decided to take the new job, it was still in the building trade but not heavy work, answering the advert in the local paper, the job was fifteen miles away in Birmingham and, after phoning for an interview, I was given a date to turn up by an Irish-sounding female voice on the other end of the phone. The office was in a small building with access up a flight of stairs from the street, upon entering there was an uneasy, restless feeling within myself to be confronted by a small Irish-speaking woman dressed all in black, one could tell by her attitude as she interviewed me that she took an immediate dislike to me, no, that's not the word, not 'interviewed' – 'questioned' is more appropriate, of my past and my experiences, she was agitated and fidgeting, she led me to the main office where the owner of the company sat at his intimidating desk, he was a good-looking chap about thirty-five years of age and he made me feel comfortable by his manner and we came to an agreement on terms and conditions of pay. The company was an old-established one with offices above and a workshop below so it was quite compact, I had to work the first few weeks with the boss's brother so he could value my worth, the boss's brother also worked on the tools, he told me he had sold his half of the company to his brother when he thought it was going under due to lack of work and money, he sold his share for £35,000 and now his brother was his boss, there were certain resentments from him over certain issues within the family but I took no notice of the smarmy quips about his brother because we all know blood is thicker than water, the other thing that struck me was the unusual camaraderie between the brother who worked and the Irish secretary who ruled and dominated the running of the company whilst Kevin, the owner-brother, sat at his desk unaware of such, and anyway he was often away golfing or spending a day at Ascot or some other social function.

Time passed and there was always a problem when the boss set on people or persons to work with this secretary, a conflict, a clash of personalities, the Irish secretary had an acerbic tongue and, although the employees were well qualified to do the job, they often ended up storming out of the office never to return, it struck me as odd that no one ever stuck the job for more than a week, Kelly, which was the Irish-speaking secretary's name, would convince Kevin of the person's incapabilities and Kevin took her word because she had been in his employ for nigh on fifteen years, it was not only the other secretaries she despised, she despised me as well for some reason, she forged a wall of mistrust between Kevin and myself and often asked me to the office to explain my actions, but. since my actions were always well intended. her accusations had no foundation once analysed and confirmed by third parties. This went on for two years, then one day an old working partner from twenty years past asked me if I wanted a job in management, well fifty-two years of age was approaching so, jumping at the opportunity of a suit, a car, expenses and no manual graft, I gave my notice in. Kevin asked to see me, we shook hands and said our goodbyes but when walking out the office and saying goodbye to Kelly she totally ignored me and never looked up. I started my new job the following week, the new company was in a state, the person who was my so-called friend had drafted me in to take the blame and pressure from him, he was married to the boss's daughter and he was a rat, we had met thirty years previous in the early seventies when working on a site with my bricklaying gang, a group of scaffold erectors had come to do a lift and amongst them was this lad, Alan, who had a beard and wore a parka to keep out the cold and was in a depressed state, on his break we sat and spoke and he told me of his dismal life and I related to it, he had just come out of Borstal and was desperate to learn a trade, we were short of men on the gang and taking a liking to him I said, 'bring a trowel with you on Monday and you can drop in on the line.' It did not take him long to learn bricklaying which is pretty easy to do after a while being very repetitive, he worked hard and was keen to learn, we spoke the same language and laughed at the same jokes and we both had a sarcastic sense humour, we became good friends and worked together for quite a few years till eventually he met this girl who was the daughter of a well-off flooring-company owner and they got married and he was drafted into the company, a kind of rags-to-riches story. Trouble is, money is never enough for a cheat and a liar, which in later years is what he became, or maybe that's what he already was the day we met - as clothes make the man, money exposes the cheat. Sitting at my desk in the same office, with Alan at one end and the owner's son at the other end as the all-seeing eye so to speak, my job was to assess insurance work such as fire and flood damage then to cost it for the insurance company and then to use the men from the company to do the work, well, the first job was to send two men to paint a kitchen in emulsion, it took them a week, one man to fix a lock one day, another to lay two slabs in another day. After confronting them and listening to their feeble excuses, I called a meeting and decided to speak with the owner's son. 'Why are you putting up with this?' was my question, 'it's a wonder you make any money.' 'We don't.' 'Right, do you want me to take charge of these men?' 'Yes,' he said. The first thing was to sack every lazy bastard in the firm, not all of them, just the lazy ones, and to ring around to people who were reliable and capable of doing the job and in two days I obtained a work force ready, in theory, to start the following week. On the Monday morning whist sitting at my desk, in walked the two sons and the owner of the company, the owner sat on my desk in front of me and looked me square in the face. 'Hope you know what you are doing,' he said to me, with a look that said, 'wrong decision – out'. 'Don't panic,' I replied. He stood up and said, 'okay,' and walked away, now there are not many people that have my respect in this life, but that man was one of them because he did not judge even though his company was in jeopardy, but he need not have worried for I am a seventh-born and live by my word, the new men turned up and the company started to function, the *status quo* between me and the boss's son became a friendship and a competition as to who could earn the most money, it was like a game and a challenge but, unknown to me, I had exposed the uselessness of Alan within the company and he decided to try to get rid of me by bad-mouthing some of my methods even though they were working - which was probably why no one took any notice. A few days later, there was a phone call from Alan whilst I was on the road, he asked me to call in on one of his clients - he had been doing private work within the company - my instruction was to pick up £3,000 in cash from the client, I refused, first, it was not my responsibility, and second, with me there is always an uneasiness with cash deals. Nothing was said about it upon my return to the office but a couple of days later things started to go wrong for Alan. Turned out he had tried to frame me — me! a seventh-born! Suddenly things he did, or had been doing, started to come to light, he had under-quoted on certain jobs and done them for a loss, money was unaccounted for, to top it all, two weeks later, upon arriving at the office, a meeting was called in front of the boss and his two sons and it transpired that Alan had been embezzling them, the client whom he had asked me to collect the £3,000 from had for some uncanny reason turned up at the office to pay the bill - which was supposed to be £13,000. Unlucky for some, unlucky for Alan, because the client said that she had already paid £10,000 direct to Alan, which only left £3,000 to pay, was that day of the phone call to pick up the money, some kind of trap set by

Pete Davies

Alan to involve me in his felonious ways? this immediately crossed my mind. Over the weekend there had been chaos within the company, on top of everything else Alan had been having an affair with another woman and had finished his marriage of thirty years that weekend exposing all his actions to his wife, the outcome was, I was summoned to the board on that Monday morning to be asked to run the company first-hand with total command, I said, 'yes,' and from that day on the company thrived, but the thing that bugs me is, after befriending a complete stranger those thirty years ago, looking after him, learning him a trade, helping him get his life back on track, watching him progress from nothing to something, I was rewarded with treachery, but treachery don't work on a seventh-born because we are immune from such things, wasn't that proof enough that what you put out in this life will return to you, and what a classic example? Time passed and the job started to get boring, it was running so well that the owner of the company told me he was thinking of retiring in two years' time and would I consider taking over the flooring business as well, but, at the same time, Kevin, my previous employer, was looking for a new contracts manager and was going into new build which was new to me and I looked upon it as a new challenge, I called him. 'Funny that,' he said, 'I've just sacked the last manager this minute and the phone has rung and it's you, come Monday for a chat.' With this under my belt, I told the other company of my intentions, they offered me more money but it was peanuts compared to their lifestyle and you can't spend thanks it won't pay the bills, not only that but the sons had married girls from the Scotland's and I had this vision of me working to keep Scotland's girls in luxury, there was no way I was going to run both companies and take the flack whilst lining the pockets of the folks who lived on the hill, with them looking down on me like a peasant, especially if the folks were born peasants like me. Arriving at Kevin's for the start of my new job as contracts manager, Kevin called me into the office. 'Pete, shut the door,' he said, 'there's something to tell you, Kelly, the office secretary, you know the one, all dressed in black, she's been to see a clairvoyant over the weekend and he's told her to beware of the initials P.D.' Well, obviously, P.D. were my initials and she had been ranting to Kevin that it would be a big mistake to employ me and it was an omen sent to her, and that he should take warning because she took this very seriously, how odd, went through my mind at the time, but now, writing this, it's plain to see that I have always misinterpreted fear for hate, the fear of being found out - remember the so-called friends who tried to poison Jean's mind towards me? How obvious now for me to see that, like Kelly, they were the losers and liars, exposing themselves to me with their own words, such is the power of the gift, but at that time never realizing or interpreting what the signs were or what they meant till it was too late, though I did have an inkling, maybe Kelly was a black witch and must have read and interpreted my sequence of numerology numbers from my application form, from my birth date, month and year, and perhaps she had checked them out with a clairvoyant or on the internet thus putting the dread and fear in her for the onset about to come, but she need not have feared me because a seventh-born is not an evil person and the only fear anyone can have is fear of the truth, the evils of this world don't trouble me, I know them well and they have no power over me, yet, inside me there is an inner power, a divine power, but it is for the good of all not for the demise that many seek, you see, you have to believe in the curses for them to work, I believe in my sequence, my number is 23/8/1947 = my life path is seven, my soul is seven, my destiny is seven, 777.

Kevin took no notice of Kelly, the week after, on my desk there was £600,000 worth of work to be processed and done, it was necessary to take work home and work late nights for nothing, knowing full well that the expectation of me was to get results and, with Kelly out of the way, it was possible to concentrate fully, all the work was late and the start and finish dates had passed, so, back in my office I set about ringing the clients and organizing new start and finish dates to which most of them agreed, the plan was for me to share the management of the workforce with Kelly, she would continue handling the day work with me doing the priced work, well there was a clash immediately, she would conflict my dates with hers and when a vehicle was needed by me she would make sure it was booked for other jobs, it was impossible to get organised and this caused conflict in which Kevin would often get involved, and she could twist a good tale could Kelly, every lie she told was cleverly worked out, and though at times she appeared right from her side I knew I was right from mine, so I decided to confront Kevin. 'Right, Kevin, there's no way it's possible to go on this way, it's not working.' 'Okay suggestions,' Kevin said. 'I need my own workforce independent of Kelly and organized access to the plant machinery.' After consideration he agreed. 'Oh by the way, Kevin, there are blank cheques lying around the office signed by you, what's that about?' 'Oh, they are left for Kelly when I am away,' was his reply, I took a deep breath, 'Kevin, not telling my gran to suck eggs, but don't ever leave a blank signed cheque with anyone, first rule of thumb in business.' The first chink in his tough armour had shown, he never retaliated in any way just gave me this pensive look as was his calm, logical mannerism, he was a clever man but had become lackadaisical due to trust, a few months later there was a moment of crisis in the office, there was no money in the company, the V.A.T. had revoked Kevin's SC60 for not paying a bill and this immediately changed the scope of the company because many of the clients did not want to deal with a company that was not V.A.T. registered, but what puzzled me was that, having completed the £600,000 worth of work backlog, chunks of money were starting to come in and yet we were still struggling as a company, I took it in my own hands to try to find out, and, because the money was starting to come in regular, Kevin decided to set on two temporary secretaries to help in the office, one was in her twenties and the other middle-aged, at first they were placed with Kelly in the same office but within a few days they were threatening to leave, Kelly was up to her old tricks with her pellets of poison, trying to make them look incompetent by misinforming them about various projects, she would raise her voice to impress Kevin who thought at the time she was a genius, stepping in one day to fight their corner, I spoke my piece to Kelly about her attitude and her bullying and took the girls under my wing by separating them from Kelly and putting them in another office and helping them obtain the correct information they needed to do their jobs, they made mistakes, as we all do, and, unknown to Kevin or Kelly, I covered for them and back-costed projects to help them when they missed out certain prices, without Kelly in their faces there was harmony. 'Stick together and Kelly can't harm you,' that was my advice to them. Days later given the keys to a back room to find a filing cabinet for my own use, I noticed there were piles upon piles of invoices, hundreds of them, some dating back ten years, ranging from £1,000 to £50,000, all day-work projects and they had not been stamped as paid, saying nothing I locked the door and carried on with my daily routine with this discovery burning away at my brain, Kevin went away the next day to some exotic place so it was not possible speak to him, it was at that time that the intuition came to me that something was wrong, it was after searching her filing cabinet for some of my invoices when I could not find them, which was one of Kelly's little tricks designed to confuse, Just think for one moment about the actions of Kelly, her own actions, it was those actions that led me to the solution that exposed her to the power of the gift, in that cabinet of hers were several of Kevin's blank cheques with my name on them, also in the cabinet there was an old Irish newspaper and who should be on the front page but Kelly, banker of the year, a full-blown picture, all dolled-up and smug, immediately I knew, my wisdom was such, it was all worked out, she was going to open an account in my name, put the cheques in a bogus bank account and, when the time was ripe, put the blame on me for embezzling the company, this was her plan to get rid of me. When she told Kevin to beware of the initials P.D. she had been confused as to who the clairvoyant was talking about, he was telling *her*, not Kevin, to beware of me. When Kevin came back the following week I confronted him with some photos taken of the cheques, he said, 'leave it with me' but never mentioned it again, meanwhile going through the invoices in the back room in secret, after ringing round many of the clients, I found that *none* of the invoices had been paid, adding them up, dating back over ten years, they came to well over £1,000,000, this was £1,000,000 due to Kevin for unpaid work, calling Kevin and suggesting a meeting, I pushed the evidence in front of him and as he read the blood drained from his face, they were all day-work invoices, Kelly had not invoiced over the last ten years, no wonder he was struggling for money and she did not want any outsiders involved, hence the saga with the secretaries. 'What shall I do? Kevin asked. 'Right, we close the company for a couple of weeks and get all the work invoiced.' We even drafted Kevin's brother in off the tools, some of the debtor companies had gone out of business so the money was lost, but some of them we were still doing work for and they must have known they had not paid their bills and they were laughing at us, there was one company we had been doing work for on a weekly basis for eight years and in all that time they had never paid one bill, it sounds unbelievable doesn't it, but it's true, eventually we recovered £400,000, Kevin made Kelly redundant, he gave her ten grand and a car, I was seething mad and said, 'why not just sack her, Kevin? 'She knows too much,' was his reply. When Kelly was gone the two girls moved into the main office, they worked well and we were a happy team, being rid of Kelly. It was about this time that Jean and I went to France to look at a property during my week's holiday but upon returning to the office things had changed, there were locks on certain doors and there was a digital lock to Kevin's office which had been used regularly by me for reference books and information, when Kevin came into the office the following day I confronted him about the locks, 'it's to keep certain people out who should not be in there,' was the reply, not thinking he meant me, I asked him for the code and when he would not divulge it, I knew immediately the Ides of March had arrived. Had the two secretaries told Kevin about our pact to help each other and probably confessed to some misdemeanour, or other, leading to this? Was it because we had a rapport in the office and the clients were addressing the mail and cheques to me as though the owner the company and we were running it well without Kevin's input? Or did Kevin decided to divide and conquer, fuelled by the demonic prophecy of Kelly which had cut deeper into his psyche than originally thought? Thus he regained control of his firm, which he had almost abandoned and had also accepted the inevitable pending doom, now it was a different story, the company was flourishing so his interest was back, he once told me that he was an avid golfer and that one could compare life to a game of golf, well, to me, golf is played by men with little balls, and sometimes by people with no balls at all, and Kevin certainly proved my point, from then on the job became a drag and, unknown to any one, Jean and I were leaving later in the year to move to France on a new adventure, and from the Ides of March onward I never bothered with any contract work to do with the firm and watched it slowly starting to slip back into the abyss. Then came the final straw. Working for the company at that time was a sneaky rat, no that's not right, a rat in rats clothing is more appropriate, like Kelly he was a yes-man, 'yes sir this, yes sir that,' a giving-you-the-finger-behind-your-back man, you know the kind we have all met them somewhere along the way, I had the measure of him from some of the men who worked for me, they often complained of him working under the influence of drugs and endangering others, he was a restless awkward person who never done no one no good but Kevin seemed to side with him like he sided with his brother, who still hated the fact that he had bailed out before the business hit the ground only to find that Kevin the pilot had pulled the doomed business up at the last moment to become the hero, and hence Kevin was riding high and flying around in cars far more expensive than the paltry thirty-five thousand pieces of silver he had bought Judas out with, the rat made tales up with the brother and, when mixed with confidences and truths confided between me and the staff, these tales became credible. One night, working late, there was a fracas in the office between the rat and one of the workforce, the argument was over a small piece of carpet off one of the jobs, Kevin's brother had told them both they could have it thus causing the problem, the incident started to get out of hand and there was a lot of pushing and shoving going on so I stepped in to calm the situation, it escalated instead, the rat took a swing at me and missed, big mistake, he was about thirty-five years of age and did weight-training judging by his physique, at fifty-four years of age and out of shape, after knocking him down the flight of stairs from top to bottom, he came back for more, knocking him down once again, he came back for more, 'right, I'm in trouble here,' went through my mind as he came at me yet again, for some reason I glanced towards cabinet on my left, on top of the cabinet was a slate-rip, the rat lunged towards me I picked up the slate-rip, which to the layman is a three-foot-long blade similar to and as thin as a samurai sword, my sword arm ready and with the blood of Arthur and Barry running through my veins my eyes were focused to the centre of his skull, my aim was to split it two inches in, dividing the nose and the lip, exiting through the bottom of the jaw, 'one more step, one pace and I swear I will split you down the middle,' was my utterance, and in that split moment it was his decision between life and death and my choice between freedom and eternal damnation, you know one can sympathize with crimes of passion and such, when that split moment arrives and that's what that moment would have been, one moment of total madness which is within us all, luckily for most people they never have to confront the demon inside of them and luckily for me neither the rat nor my demon stepped forward on that day and the situation was defused, the next day my mobile phone rang, it was Kevin informing me that the rat was considering prosecution and to apologize to him for my actions. 'No way, there's no chance me ever doing that,' was my reply. Kevin called me in to the office later and said he did not need a contracts manager anymore, well he wouldn't would he, being out of the woods? He offered me a job on the tools so he did not have to pay me any redundancy, told you he was smart - but not smart enough to see loyalty and to judge by rumours and not actions, walking out the office, past the two girls, they could not look up and face me in the eye. The firm closed seven months after on 7th January and, oddly enough, those two girls had seven days' notice, they found themselves jobless through their treachery, not only that, they will never ever have what they had again - words posed on their behalf by a special friend. These are the sort of games people play, it must take years of planning and an awful lot of skill to lie and cheat for the amount of time that Kelly did. When events like this happen they are usually man-made not coincidental, and when we can't figure things out, strange events that don't tally with normal life proceedings, you can guarantee there is a liar mixed in there somewhere, manipulating the state of play, but you can't fool a seventh-born, he can see through the facades no matter how slick.

3.

I shall be back amongst my kind.

What is it the thing that kills people's lust for life? There comes a time in many people's lives when they lose their way because their goal in life has gone and they are worn down mentally by liars, cheats and fools, and as time goes on their ambitions, no matter how small, start to fade. At the age of fifty-four change was needed in my life, there is a point you can reach which is saturation and that point had reached me, this is the time when you suddenly feel discontent, many get it around forty and go off with a younger woman or buy that Harley or get that sports car, it's a sort of regression, an attempt to start again, when all past ideals and ambitions have collapsed leaving just a shell of what you aspired to be, so the mind tries to create a new world, your new goal in life, it tells you that you have one last chance to make right the things that did not turn out as you wanted over the past years. At fifty-four years of age and starting to ask questions: 'what am I doing here; my life is being controlled by events and actions of others? Why am I such a failure? What happened to those childhood dreams of greatness promised myself when meditating encapsulated in Tommy's tomb? I did not want to be here doing this anymore. Everything in my past was born out of necessity, I loved my wife and son but needed change, needed a life too, it was at that time, when working for Kevin, that one of the men asked to speak to me, he gave me his notice and told me of his decision to change the pace and the style of his life by moving to France, trawling the internet, yes, I could build houses and make a living almost anywhere, being able to put my hands to most things, especially in a tranquil calm place away from the city, which never suited me, slowly but surely I made my plans, Jean thought I was going slightly mad but just went along with me thinking it was a midlife crisis that would just fade away, which it was but it didn't, the thing with me, I am like Ron, a doer not a talker, so I dragged Jean off to France on a couple of house-hunting trips armed with hardly any money and my schoolboy French, France became my obsession, to me it was fabulous, it had everything needed to start again, never having been there before it struck me how small the French were, no wonder we pasted them at Agincourt and Crecy, it must have been like shooting gnomes in a gallery to our bowmen, now here's a little story to amuse you, it's a popular misconception that Winston Churchill was the first to adapt the two-fingered victory sign, as any French man or historian will tell you it derives from the time of the medieval wars with France and England, when the French were able to capture an English bowman, they would cut off one of his draw fingers so he could not pluck the bow string, how they knew he was left or right handed confuses me, maybe they would hit the bowman over the head with a *mateau de bois*, thus denoting the bow hand when he went to rub the bump with an 'ouch!' or they shouted, 'who doesn't want snails or frogs legs for tea?' The English bowmen on the front line would goad the French by showing both their bow-string fingers to the oncoming hordes of French soldiers, showing that they were still able and capable of being a threat, in later years in the U.K. and America this became a crude sign to show disrespect and sometimes a good-night gesture to the boss, now in these times when the one finger is shown, little do those morons who give you the so-called finger realize that showing the one finger is telling the recipient that they are useless and as obsolete as a de-digitalised bowman and of no threat and no use at all to anyone, so, next time someone gives you the one finger so to speak, try not to burst out laughing in front of their faces, if he were alive today maybe Winston would show you the two fingers as well, especially if you told him to stop smoking and that it was bad for his health, and I can think of a lot more worse things than a baccy or a beer, such as a bullet or an arrow in the chest. We found a little cottage in Normandy and decided to buy it without even wondering where we would get the deposit; we would work that out on the way back home. As soon as we reached Blighty we put our house on the market and managed to scrounge the ten thousand quid needed as a deposit, then we had three months to sell our house in the U.K., not having much money, it was the only way. A strange thing happened when we put our house on the market, the house we were selling, as you know, was in a run-down area and having been renovated by me it stood out amongst the slums, there was also the small heated swimming pool to the rear. The estate agent who put the house on the market was somehow tied to the local newspaper, which thought there was a comical angle in that we had a swimming pool in such a run-down place, the next thing we knew a knock came to the door, it

---

was a twenty-one-year-old female reporter, she told us that her paper the *Express and Star* would like to print a story on the house because it was so unusual, we agreed, if only to give it more exposure seeing as we had to sell within the three months, not only that, A.T.V. Central News came to the door and wanted to make a short film about us which they also did, whilst talking to the reporter it somehow slipped out that I used to live on the Cannock Road as a kid. 'Funny,' the reporter said, 'that's where I live.' 'Oh yes, that's coincidental, where?' was my reply, telling her the number, she was amazed, and open-mouthed. 'That's the same address,' she said as her face changed and went solemn, 'was it a happy place, did anything untoward happen there?' she said. 'Why?' 'Well,' she said, 'since living there she had never had any luck and could not keep a boyfriend, once they had been there they never came back, also strange noises and things have happened.' Cutting her short, I said, no, it was a lovely house, not wanting to frighten her. There were many stories of bumps in the night and the latest story from Dave, was the story of the woman he met when he sold the house, according to Dave, he went out to the shops leaving this woman alone in the house, when he came back she was a wreck and jabbered on about seeing the ghost of Val rocking in her favourite chair, who got up and rushed towards her shouting, 'get out of my house! get out of my house!' Dave said he never told the woman about Val but she described Val to a tee, needless to say she never went there again, hence the move to the new flat doomed though it was, it's a pity Val didn't finish her off with the death grip, it would have saved Dave all the heartbreak, but what good would it have done to tell the reporter all this? it might have destroyed her life, made her too frightened to return to her house, and perhaps sent her on another path, spiralling through life confused, so I said nothing, she left quite content that she was imagining things, she did sell the house and move on, maybe the spirits of Tommy, Elsie and Val were still there haunting like the ghost-ships and castles of old, where spirits, having not died contently, are still trying to make the machine of life work - even in death. Dave, my brother, said that Elsie, just before her death, told him that she hated Tommy for all his doings, and it was only in his last weeks on earth that Tommy realized too late what he had got. Dave said Tommy died of a broken heart, although he had cancer of the throat probably due to the conditions he worked in and the endless fags that hung constantly from his mouth throughout his life, he died three weeks after the death of Elsie, and maybe, just maybe, his discontented spirit does wonder lost forever in the tragedy we call death, who knows? For this reason and to you all, try to put right in life what you can because a discontented life may lead to a discontented death. About both the funerals, the thing is Tommy's death was after Elsie's, but the request by Elsie on her death bed was that Tommy was not to be buried with her in the event of his death. No tears were shed for Elsie by me, in my mind she was happy, she was going to her place of rest, but for Tommy I cried excessively, Jean asked me after the funeral, 'why did you cry so much when you despised him?' Which was true although I could not answer her question at the time, on reflection, it was the relief of the finality of my past, that my past was at last truly over, and the thought of the terrible place that his spirit was destined for which was pictured in my mind.

On the 6th September 2004, with the house sold, we packed up all our belongings in a large container and left old England for our new life in Normandy, we had searched the internet and found a *gite* owned by a Welsh couple who had migrated to France one year earlier than us, and their names were Les and Russell, we had only had contact them over the net and thought they might be a couple of gays. With me always feeling awkward amongst the third gender, don't ask me why, maybe it stems from my childhood being a bit ignorant when it comes to things out of my comfort zone, I was reluctant to go but Jean convinced me that most gays are helpful and charming, taking her word, we sent the e-mail confirming our arrival and after further correspondence discovered that they were Lesley and Russell, man and wife - phew! We made our way across the channel with Spice the Doberman, two cats Luke and Leah, named from Star Wars fame, and Mr Chips the African-grey parrot, with me and Jean, all in one estate car bulging with food and enthusiasm, once we got off the ferry upon arriving at Cherbourg Docks, confusion took over, we got lost and took ten hours to get to a destination which should have taken four, we arrived at midnight at Les and Russell's property and noticed the Welsh flag they had left out to guide us to their house because it was down a dark, country lane. Upon entering the large drive and getting out of the car, this thing came towards us out of the dark, it was crouching and slurring and staggering towards us, it was Les, doubled up with drink, she walked with a stagger crouched like Groucho Marx, only with a glass in her hand not a cigar, and following behind in complete disgust and embarrassment was her mother, Audrey, anyway Les passed out so Audrey showed us to our room and left us to sleep the night, we became good friends because they were down-to-earth northerners, the sort of people we could relate to, they smoked and drank and laughed, my preference is for the company of people with all those Northern vices although I don't smoke myself now after packing it in twenty years ago. It was one of those cold winter evenings we first met, in a pub, whilst consoling Geoff Green, Dianne's ex-husband, looking across the bar there before me was the most beautiful and slender form ever, the barman introduced us, we hit it off from that moment, we left the place together and from the moment my lips touched I was smitten, we stayed together for twenty-odd years, she was always in my pocket, guiding me, helping me in times of stress, I was never without her by my side, we were inseparable, till one day when taken ill the constant nagging from her got me down, telling me how miserable life would be without her, often whispering in my ear, telling me how she could make me feel better, it was then, in that moment the realisation of the truth - she was slowly poisoning me, beneath that slim, slender form was a killer. I confronted her with questions she could not answer, she just tried to make me want her more and teased my mind, I decided there and then she was not for me and snubbed her without any notice, she begged me, tried to convince me life would be worthless without her, but, being strong, I chucked her out threw her into the street and into gutter where she belonged, at last she was gone, I missed her for a while and was tempted to relight and rekindle our relationship but stood firm, the memory of her has faded now after all those years. She has gone and good riddance, anyway Jean tells me roll-ups are cheaper, no not trollops!

Two days later, after the long, tedious engagement with the notaries and the French couple who sold it, we obtained the keys to our cottage in the country, the only thing the French couple who sold it never took was the wallpaper and that was because it was black and stuck on with super glue, we moved in on 9th September 2004, to us it was paradise, calm and tranquil overlooking the Sée valley, what a change from the hustle and bustle of the city, you could tell how time had stood still, it was like living in Fifties England with food. When we first arrived at our little cottage it was just what was needed to regain my composure, there was also a cottage next door which was ancient, dilapidated and in a bad state of repair, it had been a self-sufficient holding at one time, with cabs, carts and all sorts of farm machinery and oak beams filling the large plot. At the bottom of the garden was a large barn that must have stood for at least two hundred years in the rust and dust, one sunny day we were sitting outside our new-found haven having a cuppa and admiring the view when, suddenly, the huge barn next door collapsed with a tremendous groan, the splitting and creaking of two hundred year old oak beams was deafening, it had waited those two hundred years to cease in that moment in time to be witnessed by us, now I have always had this sort of intuition that Jean has some sort of mystic powers of seeing, people have often hinted as much, asking her opinion when strange happenings have occurred but never really saying the reasons why, but it is true that on occasion she does see the faces of the dead which often come to her in visions, but they never speak to her. maybe she has to take that one step further, when we first met she would often tell me of her interest in Mystical things but I always deflected her from that path knowing full well of my own experiences, I suppose it was the fear of the unknown at that point of my life, I did not want to open something I could not and did not understand at that time. Anyway my mind is made up that, to put up with me, she must be on the same path as me, and this is one of the reasons we were attracted to each other those many years ago, often I have fought her cause and I am sure that unknown to me on many occasions she has fought mine. Here's something strange to puzzle your minds, there has often been times when both of us have walked passed certain objects, boxes and clothes-racks in supermarkets and shops, to find that, for no reason at all, some things tend to shoot off the shelves, not directly to the ground but across our path, one time a clothes-rack full of clothes shot straight across the aisle right in front of us, we put this down to static energy - dowsing is one of my skills and watches won't work on me because my body often gets charged which can result in a sharp electric shocks when touching metal objects – and we class these happenings as unexplained phenomena, it happened again the other day at a supermarket, a box shot off the shelf in front of me when no one else was around, Jean came round the aisle and saw me smiling at the box on the floor, she never said anything because we class this as a normal happening, maybe this phenomenon stems back to the early days spent in incarceration fasting and meditating at Tommy's leisure, often I would sit for days trying to move objects with my mind, I knew I could do it, it was just that they never moved, and I knew I was a genius, it was just that no one else did, I was certain that, as my life progressed, I would be wealthy beyond dreams but never was, it's as though all of my hopes passed me by, many times teetering on the brink of wealth, my fingertips touching but never quite reaching it, my first experience of this was when walking down a back-country lane from the tip at the age of seven, in a ditch to the side of the road was three black bags, two were tied but the third was spewing out what looked to me like silverware, there was at least one tankard and one goblet on full view, the goblet looked like a Holy Grail and was encrusted with what might be jewels. 'Shall I pick it up?' I asked myself, but fear and righteousness told me not to, so I hurried back home to speak to Ron for his advice and opinion, but the wise one was not there, bubbling in my mind were avarice and greed, telling me to go back, grab a piece and grab it fast, upon returning, just one hour later, all had gone.

We had been in France about six months, it was about this time Jean started to get a pain to her groin, she had a constant temperature and often complained of pins and needles to her head, said she had no feeling in her fingers. In England a couple of years before we went to France, it was normal for me to come home from work in the middle of the winter and the windows and doors would be wide open, we thought she was in the change, you know, the sweats and all that, we should have read the signs but we trusted the judgment of the British doctors which was a big mistake.

We registered with the doctor in the little French village we lived near, and I made an appointment, Jean said she would come with me just for a check-up and we both attended the doctor who gave me a blood test for new tablets for gout, he then proceeded to give Jean an overhaul, her blood pressure was at a ridiculous high of two hundred and forty over one hundred and ten, and it was causing the pins and needles to her face, Dole, which was the French doctor's name, said she needed tablets right away to reduce the blood pressure, she could have a stroke at any time, so she was given tablets to reduce this and they worked, but the pains persisted in her groin and in June 2005 she was tested for many things, to no avail, and was then admitted to a polyclinic, which is sort of a private clinic, for a scan, but the scan resolved nothing, the French, unlike British doctors in my experience, never gave up or passed it off as they did in England, they offered Jean a colonoscopy but the camera could not pass the bowel, next day she was given a barium meal and the results of the X-rays showed a large portion of her colon was rotted away, one would assume that if this happened, septicaemia would have set in months before and would normally have resulted in death, but no, we were called into the cancer ward for the results of the X-rays. We sat down. 'It's not cancer is it?' said Jean. 'Highly likely,' said Doctor Marron, the cancer specialist, everything stopped in time at that moment, it was the ultimate fear and dread, but the shadow of death had only shown his hand and the cards had only just been dealt and the game had only just begun. The things you need to confront death are courage and strength, a bit of luck and, probably, defiance, let him know he has a fight on his hands, show him no respect and don't throw your cards in before the end of the game, within a week we were on our way to surgery for a long and complicated operation which a few years earlier would not have been possible, in a foreign land the complications were immense, most of the nurses refused to speak any English to Jean even in times of severe pain, Jean was in pain and under stress and in tears, once, when she needed to move due to bed sores, an auxiliary told the nurse to tell her to run around like a headless English chicken although the ward sister, who was very kind and thoughtful and did speak some English, reprimanded the auxiliary, telling her that Jean could speak some French and understood, another time, when Jean needed some help to go to the toilet, the nurse shouted *parlez-vous Francais*, repeatedly, screaming insanely like Hitler at a Nuremburg rally, so don't tell me about French nurses and compassion - on the other hand the surgeons were a complete opposite and were very helpful, suppose it was because they were educated.

The operation was a success they removed five cancerous polyps, the trouble was, they put you in a recovery room after the operation and, when you come round, pain killers are given based on the decibels of your screams and not before, strange but that's the French method, with fifty-nine stitches from top to bottom of her torso and her insides cut and stirred about, Jean's pain was tremendous and the screams horrendous because no pain killers were given at that time, the twelve days in hospital passed very slowly for her, on the fifth day she started feeling better and asked the surgeon if she could go home, he looked at her sternly and in his broken English said, 'do you want to die? Do you realize the extent of your operation?' This calmed her to face the rest of the internment, then after the operation she had to face the prospect of chemotherapy for six months, in another branch of the hospital where the nurses were totally robotic, but, to be fair, this was a rural area in the backwoods of Normandy, not Paris. We had won the first hand and left death cursing his luck and probably going on to challenge and search for a weaker victim. The chemo was hard for Jean, she lost her hair and had strange feelings to her limbs and when she touched anything it was as though she was getting electric shocks, and she was generally sluggish, the reason for this was that no one had picked up that she was also a diabetic, also unknown to us at the time, which was confirmed after they gave her a few tests, they changed her chemo dosage to a chemical called Folofox which made a tremendous difference. After she came out of hospital, the nurses came to the house every day for twenty days to clean the stitches and remove them, that is how the system works in France but you have to get your own nurse because they are all private individuals, eventually Jean gathered strength but she had lost an awful lot of weight, it takes about six months to get back on your feet after such a trauma but we were only glad it was over and the cancer eradicated, or so we thought, for a few months life was good, then, after the six month scan, another polyp was discovered, the excuse was, 'you grow polyps quickly, this particular polyp was in an out of the way, awkward place, unable to be reached with keyhole surgery', another operation was on the cards, it was that or a life expectancy of six to twelve months, we sat at the table of death again, awaiting the deal from the deck that was stacked against us, this time the odds were shortening and death was rubbing his hands, knowing full well that this time he had a good chance of winning, but what death did not know was that Jean had an ally, someone who knew him well and had faced him on a couple of occasions, we both pulled together and summoned our inner strengths to confront the second operation, which was an exact repetition of the first except this time no chemo was needed and without chemo things were a lot easier. Once again, Jean gritted her teeth and braved the trauma and survived, now anyone would think that Fate would say 'this is enough for any person to suffer,' but no, *another* operation was needed because the rest of her colon was in trouble, any lesser person would not have coped with this but Jean is a determined soul and once she decides there is no stopping her, she said she wanted to be here for a few more years, to feel the breeze and sun on her face a while longer and to hold on to this precious life, so she went ahead for her third colostomy in five years, and there was an added problem, she also needed a reservoir putting in her chest, this is like a small, plastic port to allow endless needles to be inserted to save collapsing her veins which had become collapsed after all the previous operations, she told me that she was conscious while the doctors did this, they came into the operating theatre, put some sort of bubble-wrap silver around her left side and legs then barked 'cold, cold', in cold-hearted French, then the whole side of her body went numb and they made an incision in the left side just below her shoulder, 'turn right, turn right,' the surgeon shouted as he hammered port in with a small mallet then stitched it up, sounds like something out of a science-fiction film, doesn't it? Jean has often told the British doctors of this and they looked at her dismissively as though she's nuts. The wound had to heal and she was sent home, but a month later she had to return for another major operation, after this third time there was no colon left so to speak, although the surgeon said the operation had been difficult but successful, but we weren't to throw our cards in yet, the game was not over, there was one final twist of fate, we had a nurse attend the after-care who thought more of her appearance than her job and the stitches went septic and started to open up and caused a hernia, poor Jean had to suffer another visit to the hospital to get the hernia corrected. Having no colon changes your life dramatically and you have to plan your life toilet-orientated because in France they don't think it is necessary to give you a bag.

A year passed, and our next visit to the specialist was due, we were told that nothing was inevitable, and the box implant was to remain in Jean's chest for the rest of her life due to the fact that it would make treatment easier should complications occur or the cancer return at a later date, we left the specialist with all this in mind, that day we sat on a river bank in the town, the time and tide flowing past, and the calmness was a sort of revelation for both of us, we talked and decided that, due to the fact that Jean's diabetes was not under control and she had an infection from the last operation which was not being resolved, and because the general after-care was poor and the French were unhelpful, we decided we would sell everything, buy a motor-home and hit the road back to England where we could understand

and explain our situation. We were not confident, when we left the U.K. in 2004, Jean had complained of these pains for two years previous, she had had tests and had stayed in hospital overnight and the diagnosis had been gastro problems but nothing cancerous, but the French had discovered that she had had this cancer for about three years before we arrived in France and that this had resulted in the rotted colon - the sweats, the pins and needles and the blood pressure had been obvious signs - so we were going back into a cauldron of confusion. To anyone, should you have any pain constantly, this is a warning, don't let anyone persuade you different, doctor or no, take no notice of those so-called television doctors quoting from an instruction leaflet inside a box so they can be on the box who are too frightened to commit themselves, Jean's pain started in the groin and we have often heard people complain of this, first go to your doctor and get a colonoscopy, insist now, it could save your life, never, never, never take no for an answer. When we left the U.K. in 2004, the National Health was in a pathetic state, long queues, waiting hours on end, the fact that Jean's mom went into hospital for a minor problem and contracted septicaemia in there and died within weeks did not help our confidence, however, on returning to the U.K. after six years, we were amazed at the professionalism of all the nursing staff at New Cross hospital in Wolverhampton and at the after-care, and at the time of this writing they are far superior to anything the French can offer. Death doesn't challenge us anymore, because he knows he can't win at this moment in time, but he will be back to chance his hand again, and one day our luck will run out but not this day or this time, and not on his day or his time, we will choose when we decide to leave this world, it's not for him to decide, you see, he only comes when he senses he can win, when we are low we drop our defences and become vulnerable and weak, in times of trouble keep strong, believe in yourself, above all you must believe and have a belief that's more powerful than death itself and then death has to pass you by, but don't fear, because death is the end of this life and the start of the next, someone once said that the only two things in this life that are certain are taxes and death, well the first has been proven wrong by the greedy and the second will be proven wrong by the meek, and it depends on what you call death, if it's likened to the discarding of the caterpillar and the chrysalis then it is so, but from that empty shell shall bloom another beautiful life one of freedom, a spirit life. Have you noticed, you never see a dead butterfly unless it has been trapped in the web of this life, well it's the same with the human spirit.

Within six months we did as we had planned on that river bank, we purchased the motor home and sold the house to a Parisian couple. In France it takes three months to tie up the legal side, we sold the house in June and by September we were on the road, there was one small glitch, amongst all the confusion and hospital visits and selling the house we had not arranged for the rabies vaccine for the animals and we were tied up for a further six months before we could return to England, we were minus Spice the Doberman and Chips the African Grey but plus one little Jack-Russell-cross fox terrier named Smudge, a few months before we left, Spice, our Doberman had reached the age when her legs had gone, she was ten and there were many painful and sleepless nights for me knowing her time had come, one day she sat in her own urine and faeces and could not get up, at that moment I made my heart-breaking decision, it was her time, remembering the pact we had when we fought together against the demons of this world, holding her in my arms and singing her favourite song, John Lennon's, *All You Need Is Love*, she slipped away under the injection at the vets, writing this the tears come flooding back even after the years, any dog or animal lover will know the pain, but from the death of Spice came the life of Smudge and we love him and hope that when his time comes we are still here to do the responsible thing, Jean's African Grey, Mr chips was his name, which she loved as much as Spice, also passed away just a few weeks before we were due to leave France, we had some wonderful times with them, they were part of the family, we had taught Chips to say many things, I would sing *Love me Tender* and after a couple of lines he would say, 'are you Elvis?' we also taught him the John Lennon song *All You Need Is Love*, after whistling and singing 'love, love, love' he would say, 'it's easy' and then carry on the chorus again, we often put him outside in his cage and one day Philippe and Michelle, our neighbours, had a July-the-Fourteenth Bastille-Day party, there were about fifty guests, all relatives of theirs, both of us were sitting at the top of the garden chatting and we saw the guests starting to congregate at our fence, we walked over to them and as we approached the fence we could hear 'love, love, love' it was Chips whistling and singing to them, what fascinated them was, if you listen to the opening bars of the song it is a similar tune to the Marseilles, the French national anthem, and, it being Bastille Day, the French loved it, and for years after groups of children with their parents would visit our little cottage just to see Chips do his party piece, not only that, we taught him to speak some French, those African Greys are so intelligent it does not take long for them to learn, but they only say what you teach them, we think he fell and broke his wing, we tried to get a bird vet in France but to no avail, we hoped we would get him back to the U.K. but he just got weaker and weaker, then one day Jean held him in her arms sang 'love, love, love' to him and he passed on, we cremated him, held his ashes to the wind and he was gone,

On the 9th September 2010 we left Normandy behind, said goodbye to our couple of friends and headed for Portugal for the six months with the two Bengal cats and Smudge, we could do this even though we had not got the rabies injections cleared because the injections are just for the U.K. - we could not enter the UK without putting the animals in six months' quarantine. The cats, who we thought were going to be the problem, were brilliant, we let them out in the day and they had the intelligence to come back at night for food and bed. Smudge on the other hand was trouble, we nearly lost him on a couple of occasions, last time we lost him it was for fifteen hours, he chased a wild cat, pulled the lead out of my hand and ran into a nearby wood, I searched all night for him, after several hours, I heard a whimper but it was hard to distinguish a direction and it was dark and pouring with rain, after fifteen hours of searching I was about to give up ever finding him and returned back to the motorhome for something to eat, but whilst cooking some breakfast a voice came into my head, 'go to this place', it said, I dropped everything, Jean said, 'where are you going?' Breakfast was half cooked. 'Finish that off for me, I will be back soon,' I replied and headed to the place planted in my mind, shouting, 'Smudge, Smudge,' whilst searching through the dense undergrowth, I was just about to walk away when, 'woof, woof,' - two distinct barks, weak but definite - they pointed me in a direction, digging through weeds and nettles I came to a large branch which blocked the way, I made my way around this obstacle and there in full view, with un-wagging tail, soaking wet and disorientated, was a Smudge-type dog with the lead wrapped tight round his neck and entangled in the branches of a fallen tree. 'He'll do,' I thought to myself, I picked him up and took him back to the motorhome, dried him out and warmed him up with some hot bone soup, now he is back to his old ways, a blinking pest, but we still love him, having passed that area within feet of him it must have been twenty times in the night, from every direction, shouting and calling, to no avail, it seems odd to me that he was in that place, the moral is: don't give up even though the situation looks hopeless, keep going till you get a conclusion, and have faith in your guardian angel.

We approached the Pyrenees and Jean suggested we make a detour and go to Lourdes, it was only a few hours away, we approached Pyrennees and the mountains were awesome to us, we had never seen anything similar or felt so humbled before, when we arrived at the base of the mountains just outside Lourdes, we found a campsite to stay at for a few days and, when we entered the site, a lone man stood by a small caravan which had obviously been stationary for a while, it was in such a dilapidated condition, this strange feeling came over me that he was somehow troubled and that we would be involved with him, or that he might even be a problem, he was about thirty years of age with long, blonde, flowing hair tied back in a ponytail and with piercing blue eyes, he wore only a pair of shorts and his torso was weathered and tanned a golden brown, we started to park our motor home and, sure enough, he came over to us and said, 'you can't park here, you're blocking my view,' the view being a fantastic panorama of the Pyrenean Mountain Range, with a slight anger to his tone, he repeated, 'you're blocking my view.' He stared at me direct into my eyes for what seemed a while then took a sharp step back and said, 'look you can park over there,' which was just at the back of his caravan and not blocking his view. 'Okay,' I said, and parked and proceeded to talk to him, he had lived this lone existence for five years, I asked him why he was here and other friendly banter to which none of my questions he replied to, we sat and chatted and spoke of Jean's plight and our plans and my plans for writing this book about the seventh-born, we laughed and left each other amicably. The next day, deciding to go to town, out of nowhere stepped this man, on a road crossing on an otherwise empty street, forcing me to stop abruptly. Beeping my horn and putting my thumb up to him, I said to Jean 'don't think he noticed me,' after he never acknowledged me, anyway we carried on, did our shopping and went back to the site, then, late in the evening, about eleven o'clock, we had decided to go to bed when a knock came to the motorhome door, it was the man from the caravan. 'I must speak with you,' he said, standing in the darkness, 'please, let me speak with you,' he pleaded, he was insistent. 'Okay, come in and sit down - what is it?' 'We met again today on the crossroads,' he said, 'it was then I knew.' 'Knew what?' 'It's you, you're the one sent to help me.' I felt confused but he began to speak with a calmness that settled me, in the same calmness that Elsie spoke, 'I am the Archangel Gabriel,' he said, another alien I thought to myself, scanning his hand to see if he had a funny fag going, had he not spoken with such an air of mystery and calmness I would have been worried but I wasn't, we sat opposite each other in the dim lighting of the motorhome and he told me of the disaster he had seen in Phuket where hundreds of his friends had been killed, had he not decided on that fatal day to visit a friend on higher ground he would have been amongst them and would have been able to save some of them, he told me of the aftermath of the horrors, of body parts everywhere whilst holiday makers bathed in the sun amongst the dead on the beaches, his once friends, his deep blue eyes were piercing me as he spoke, I could sense the heaviness and sadness in his heart, his head slumped to one side as though the anguish of the memories was too much to bear, it was almost as though he had fallen from grace, he looked hungry. 'Would you like something to eat?' I said, 'yes,' he said, we ate some bread and sipped some soup together, we spoke of the good and the bad in this world and he told me of his sorrow for this holy place of Lourdes, the Mecca of millions of the infirm and crippled, the shops adorned with figures of plastic gods that glowed in the dark, with statues and crucifixes and anything that man could think of to draw the poor hopefuls towards this place of belief, was he searching for the answer too? He told me that when he passed through the large gates of the religious place it was how he had imagined it would be, leaving greed and hypocrisy behind - but greed and hypocrisy were within. He walked up to the basilica passing all nationalities, all hoping to find some sort of solace, but he felt nothing, he walked under the central dome which was a glass-stained mosaic decorated like the tips of a peacocks feathers, it was as though a thousand eyes were watching him, when he past the confession boxes he had nothing to confess, he turned the corner of the Disneyland church and there before him was the life-giving water, people were filling plastic bottles through dozens of taps, no doubt put there by some water company, to one side was a cave with a statue of a woman dressed in religious clothing, hundreds of people filed past to kiss or touch the rock beneath, if some of them had not an illness when they went in, there would be quite a few who would come out with some bacterial infection or other, after that there was the candle-burning grotto, where you buy a candle for ten euros and burn it for your dead, he said that anyone hoping for a miracle cure, came out exactly as they went in, well, as for me, some may call me a sceptic, you see I don't work for any of those religions and they don't work for me, you can only be punished or cured if you are a member. However, in spite of all the things Gabriel told me, 'my advice to anyone is to visit this beautiful place at the foot of the Pyrenees whatever your reasons,' as for me, I am content to have met Gabriel and to leave that place with fond memories and the little bottle of holy water Jean managed to get — well! you never know do you. We left the next day and said our goodbyes to Gabriel and we also left a happier more contented person behind than the one we met, it was as though he had got all that was past behind him and could talk of a positive future, he said he was going back to find his place in time, and said some day through fate we would meet again. I learned something from Gabriel, he said I was naïve, which was true but not realized by me at the time, and angry, which was still true at the time, and he taught me humility amongst many other things, and not only that, he learned me to text on my phone, so you see, that chance meeting between two negatives formed a positive and we have both come out of this with a smile and a sort of mind-cleansing. Have you ever taken that deep breath and your body is totally relaxed? Well, that's the thing, and now it's possible for me to start this book with all the gifts given to me by the Archangel Gabriel. One last thing, when we said our goodbyes he adorned Jean with a white cheap luminous plastic beaded crucifix, the type one would see in the local religious shops around Lourdes, 'wear this and keep your faith and keep strong,' he said, and to me he gave a white card, 'what's your real name by the way I said?' 'Jannel.' was his reply, sticking the card in my pocket with a smile, and saying, 'if ever you need me just call me,' a few weeks later the card which I had forgotten about dropped out of my pocket, Ganel International, that was all that was on the pure glossy white card no telephone number, no address, and no e- mail, now if you look close at the name Ganel, hmmmmm I wonder?

Relating to the Phuket incident, when we were about to move over to France to live in 2004, we answered an advert in a local car mart to purchase an estate car, phoning the seller who lived in Coventry Jean and I made our way over there by train, when we arrived at the house there was a for-sale sign in the garden. 'Oh, you're selling.' 'Yes,' he said, 'we want to move to France but we're not sure how to go about the procedure.' 'That's odd so are we.' He called his wife over and for one split second in her company there was a feeling of uneasiness within me as she spoke, shrugging this off, they invited us in and asked us to come to tea the following week, which we did because we had to pay for and collect the car, they learned a lot about France from us, within two weeks they had purchased a property via the internet not far from where we were going to live, they stopped with us in Normandy the following Christmas and used us as a base to establish themselves, it was the time of the Phuket disaster which happened years before we met the Archangel, we were watching the disaster unfold on the TV and the woman said to me, 'if we had not have met you, we were going there this Christmas for a holiday, when we go back to the U.K. we will get a booking there right away because it will be cheap due to the disaster.' What inhumanity, those were perhaps two of the people who were sitting amongst the dead that the Archangel spoke about and, needless to say, they dumped us once they had established theirselves in France and our usefulness had expired. These are the sort we all have to be aware of, the parasites of this world, the ones who will suck your life blood in order to survive. We had decided to head back to England after Christmas to arrive in the U.K. about March which would be the end of the six month's quarantine for the animals, it was a good thing it happened that way, the winter in England was severe and existence in a motor home would have been difficult to say the least, we did not want to travel any further through Spain because we had met several English couples who had been robbed when passing through the cities, one couple told us they were on a large traffic island and they heard a hissing noise, they got out of their motorhome to find a flat tyre, they had just enough time to see someone flash past on a scooter, while they were checking the tyre a Spaniard came over to them, told them they could not stay there and he would help them but this was just a ploy whilst the third person of the scam was in the back of the motorhome stealing all their valuables, we had also experienced a couple of hairy moments ourselves which Smudge alerted us to, if anyone is creeping around at night Smudge knows about it, no matter how quiet they are.

On all Fool's day 2011 we landed in England and headed towards the Midlands to start the process of getting Jean's problems finalized, the long process of getting registered has started and we have got the ball rolling so to speak, and we are currently on a farm site, we have now been on the road for eighteen months, we love it and don't think we are ever going to buy another property, just travel, why go into debt at our age? We have many plans and have met many people on the road, some nice, some not worth mentioning, we have been invited to Germany, Holland, Spain and even Australia - amongst many other places - but would the Motorhome make it? We met a couple who said to us, we don't know how you can do this full time, what's going to happen when you reach old age, or when one of you is taken ill, well we're not spring chickens and what can be worse than Jean's trauma, and when we do reach an age when we can't do this anymore that will be the day we will choose to die, not locked up in some room, a lonely old couple awaiting for some miracle to happen, we said to them, 'why do you come away for weekends in your caravan?' 'For the peace and quiet, the tranquillity and we love it,' they said, well so do we, full time, anyway this Motorhome is our life-pod. Jeans cancer has now gone, though she has to contend with side effects and takes lots of pills, she takes them daily and tips them on the table and it reminds me of a pay-out jackpot on a Vegas slot machine, there are that many, and with diabetes her body will never be the same as when she was young, she now has no colon and no womb because she had a hysterectomy at the age of forty, her gallbladder has to come out and the British doctors are going to remove a goitre to her neck and also the portacath that was used for chemo in France, at this moment in time she has to have it flushed out every month in a hospital, which is awkward in foreign countries with the language barrier, although they don't charge to do it, except the British hospital in Gibraltar where it cost £150, the alternative was 'tough luck', if you didn't have the money and we would have had to go back to the Spanish, French or Portuguese to get the lifesaving treatment even though Jean is a pensioner. I'm not going to bother renewing her passport, just take her out the country one piece at a time, what matters to us most you see, is that we remember all the things we planned when we were young, and we remember the hopes and dreams of Jean's parents which never materialized after they had struggled hard all their lives, and all of the things they ever wanted in this life had passed them by, we nearly left it too late ourselves to see the world together. To those of you adventurous budding maniacs out there, my advice is, don't wait till you retire, believe me, when you reach our age the aches and pains will suppress you somewhat, get rid of the kids, marry them off as soon as possible and go as early as you can whilst you still have your health and courage. We have many things to do and see and the world has many things to offer us in return and many secrets to divulge, some would call it the bucket list, well the bucket is quite full at the moment and we have now closed this one chapter of our lives to start the next, we have forgotten fantasy and ignored reality in order to live our dream.

When looking back at the opening lines of this book I realise I was searching for an answer when deciding to write it, and I may have found one, none of these ideas occurred to me till reading here amongst my own writings, still don't know my past, meaning my family history, there were never any photos or documents of Tommy or Elsie's past lives, what few documents that were left were destroyed by Dave when he left the house. No matter, this book is the key to some of the questions often asked by myself and it's strange, you never see some things till they are laid out in front of you and you have put all the pieces together, it's as though I have been waiting all my life for this moment to arrive, and each page is a piece of a jigsaw, unveiling the prophecy Elsie spoke of, the prophecy of freedom, happiness and contentment, the reason I see things different, the prophecy which released me from the same chains that bound her in misery. Was this the message Elsie was trying to tell me: to seek the truth and justice will follow? To tell it, preach it, speak it and breathe the message and word of justice for the rest of my days? Did Elsie see the future and with her wisdom know how to break the shackles that bound me and, to free me, told me of this gift? Told me that through my life I would never be rich but also would never want? Do not the stories of bankruptcy and the legacy left by Eric portray this? The story of the building company is a parable because justice does prevail against the liars and cheats and the vile - come to think of it, the word vile is an anagram of 'evil', and so is mantle to 'lament'. When writing of the cross that changed into a sword, was the destruction of the sword by Tommy an act of spite? Or was it misinterpreted by me, was it an act of fear? And were Tommy's hate and lies also misinterpreted by me? Was it the fear of what he knew that made him so callous and cruel? There has to be a reason. Was it the cross which Tommy feared which made him act so, the cross of justice, the power of the sword that brought strength and defiance where there was weakness? Ron, my brother, took the path of the cross and I took the path of the sword, aren't they the same, didn't we fight the crusades under the same symbols, the cross and the sword, in the name of truth righteousness? And was Tommy's destruction of the sword irrelevant because the symbol and legacy of the sword and the cross were never destroyed, the symbols of justice and freedom? Was the cupboard on that night keeping me awake to defend myself and my family and face the evil that was present on that particular occasion? And was it an angel, a demon, or even an alien that cast the shadow on the window that fearful night. Suffering from gout from time to time, the pain always comes between the times of the full moon, keeping me awake through the long nights of agony spent howling beneath the silvery glow, but my doctor told me there was nothing wrong with me and refused to give me anything for it, is this the prophecy of the werewolf? Did death spare me on occasion - or did my angel protect me to tell this story? To bring this message? Were the foundries of hell there for me to be tested and shown my inevitable path of evil, to curb me from the dark side which, unknowingly I was entering by wishing ill on those despised by me, only to find that in later life that those evils had come back to me tenfold trying to destroy the only person I ever loved, repaying my deeds in the form of Jeans illness? When visiting the holy place suggested by Jean, was the Archangel there to comfort me and teach me compassion, to curb the bitterness forged in my mind from the early days which has now gone? Had that bitterness cloaked the reality which, at this time, is plain for me to see? Is the reason for this book to make me see, to make you see? To humble me? Writing this has solved the puzzle, my puzzle, the reason I am as I am. Some may say I analyse too deep, some may say I am mad, on one hand there seem to be times of insanity but on my other hand there is normality, nothing in my writings suggests about the gift of healing, the one gift that really matters to me, is this book a message for me to try? Do I have that gift having lived all of the other prophecies from Elsie, take for instance the severe pains suffered by me for twenty years, and also Jean's eradicated cancer, ask yourselves how come Jean survived when so many have died from the same illness, one could say it is coincidence or even luck that she recovered so well, but, believe me, I summoned all my inner powers of persuasion and opened many of the doors on those two occasions, luck never came into it, it's more faith, the question is: should Elsie's message inspire me to go out into the world and along the way to try to help needy and good people? To try the healing hand if the opportunity rises? To see if it is possible to do some good for a change? It is not possible for a seventh-born to benefit from the gift, it is for others, but perhaps it may make the thieves, the liars, the vile and the cheats of this world think twice before they ply their trade, for fear of the retribution to come, not surmising from some ancient book that no one believes in or understands, these are the words of my findings over my years, they are modern-day truths, we will all go back to Mother Earth in our final days but, remember, below the surface of the earth, far below, is a fiery mantle where you may lament, trapped in spirit for all time. Do you really know where you come from? Where you are going back to? When you stand before your god, don't think the words 'was led and influenced by others, and misguided'. will hold any credibility, it is for you and you alone to decide, now you have read the writings of this book, see if it changes you for the worse or if it fuels good and common sense in your mind, be your own judge, maybe this book will inspire you to seek what you are looking for, your answer, there are people like me who already know who they are and where they are going but some are too frightened to speak out because others may ridicule them when they do not conform to the stereotype they have been moulded into. Here I have bared myself to every crank, liar and cheat in this world, I don't care, they are nothing to me, these are my beliefs and I know them to be true, anyway it would be unwise for such persons to goad or try to ridicule a seventh-born, would you not agree? Don't be afraid of vicious words, they mean nothing, actions are far more powerful and the pen is not mightier than the sword, although, without them both, this message could not be passed on. I often have this dream of floating across a large expanse of calm stillness, as though drifting through a galaxy of stars, circled by twelve tall gigantic majestic wraith figures standing like great kings, as they beckon me I see myself from high above in an eagle's-eye view, approaching their cosmic centre, my strength leaves me and the light of the sun and world fade to distance, with my soul descending and melting amongst the warm comforting shades from which there is no return, calmly and serenely accepting my lot, judged by that greater power, this is the way I will leave this life, a fighter to the end, but ready for the next. Succumbing to the inevitable, you will find my wandering spirit midst deepest oceans, by darkest ancient forest lakes, on bleakest haunting misty moors, in sunsets on golden shores, with shimmering ripples at water's edge, I shall leave no stain upon this earth, no chiselled stones need state my worth, no tears for me, I shall be free, no fence, no boundary, no lock, no key. Look to the stars, I shall be gone in spirit-wind to become the driven soul that breaks the boundaries of evermore, and, should you hear phantoms skipping on the run, we shall do no har m to anyone, just passing time with ancient friends and recollections of past reflection, and when you too are finally laid to rest within that field of velvet dreams, perchance to hear a haunting melody, don't pay it any mind come join and see, that from where the shadowy sun sets within those casted echoes you will find no thought of regret or sorrow.

Postscript

The date is the 30th of September 2011, we have been in England now for five months, Jean has had practically every scan in the medical dictionary, the findings are that the cancer is eradicated although she still has to attend hospital every month for the port wash to the chemo box implanted by the French, we had a scare a couple of weeks ago, she developed pains to her abdomen and lay in bed for five days in pain, we now have this golden rule since the nightmare of the weird wolf incident - that when either of us get any concerning illnesses, we sit it out for the three days and if, after that, it still remains, it's the hospital, in this case we did the wrong thing, her gallbladder became infected, I had to take her to Accident and Emergency, they did some tests and admitted her, she was in a tremendous pain, it turned out to be trapped gallstones and, according to the specialist, this was another product of having no colon, and I had another scare, thinking that she might not recover, in those few valuable minutes we held hands and she told me to continue to live my dream, that she may not be here tomorrow. Her blood levels started to plummet dangerously low, panicking the nursing staff and resulting in a couple of doctors doing emergency treatment, but eventually she was stabilized and now all is well, the thing that made me laugh was, when she was delirious and everyone was panicking, tubes hanging everywhere, telly screens bleeping warnings, with all the doctors around testing this and testing that, she sat up in bed induced by morphine and said, 'I know what's wrong with me, you are feeding me pure oxygen and my body can't cope with the purity, I need a fag to compensate.' The situation was serious but I burst out laughing, much to Jean's displeasure, she barked at me, 'who are you laughing at? It's not funny.' 'Well you're not having a fag,' said the nurse which Jean accepted, just goes to show the power of the weed. She was kept in hospital for several days after and now has to face an operation to have the gallbladder removed at some time in the near future along with the goitre and the chemo line, her constant bowel problem may soon be eradicated, we have only the diabetes problem to solve now and she can start to live a pretty reasonable existence, the doctors and specialists have taken a great interest in Jean's history and have told her how interesting it is for them to follow her progress.

Meanwhile, Dave still lives in his tower block far from the world of reality, he doesn't want to go out anywhere and says he is happy doing nothing; he rings me often to tell me he loves me, as I love him. And, at the time of writing this paragraph, Marlene and Arthur are still going strong, she is eighty-four and Arthur is eighty-one and he has dementia, it may be the payback for that brain-scrambling blow he gave me on that November night when my mind cursed him for the pain, when asked about the past, he says he can't remember some things, maybe he does but won't admit it, or maybe he has inherited a poor memory from his boxing days as many ex-boxers do. Marlene often gets on to him and nags him because he has lost interest in all things, he sits around watching telly whenever she allows him to, when odd jobs need doing she has to pay someone to do them. I said to him only the other day, 'how come you can't remember a lot of things?' He said, 'because it's easier not to', such is Arthur.

Ron is still alive and well, a few years ago one of his old acquaintances said to me, 'sorry about Ron getting killed in the late Sixties', apparently the rumour had got around that he had been run over by a car, next time I visit his house I will check the greenhouse to see if there is a large pod in there, after all, I said it myself - when he left England for a while in the Sixties that he came back a changed man, practically unrecognizable from the old Ron, no Black-Country accent either, all his kids have flown the nest and all are well educated and have good jobs, he became a systems analyst in later years and earned good money, now he is retired. Most of the time when I see him he tries to steer me in the right direction but that's his direction, I am sure that when he reads this he will see he has nothing to worry about, we both have the same views, fly the same flag, and believe in the same things - just from different perspectives, it's just that I was cast upon stony ground and it took a while to find my way into the sunlight.

Martin, our lad, trundles on with his business though the times are hard for anyone with an ideal, the world has changed and I'm glad that the likes of me can retire and look back, not envying any young person having to live through this present era, they have to carry the burden of responsibility now that they are the current generation, I am sure that every generation that passes looks back on the new one and is glad it's not them and I' sure it will be the same for Martin when his time comes to retire

As for me, well now my task is done, I feel this is the reason I am here on this earth, to give you all this message whether you believe it is entirely up to you, the one thing you do have left is your power of choice and decision, no one can take that away or manipulate it, it's yours. I feel now I can finish my life as I choose so that's what I intend to do, there are no chains binding me, no guilt and no remorse for what might have been, so it's off on my travels to have a look round this planet to see if it was all worth it, and I am sure it will be, because when I meet one good person my heart lifts and it gives me confidence that you, the peacemakers, the gentle and the meek, will inherit the future.

When looking back, I would like to think that Geoff could have been my true brother and I could have been the son of Freddy Alcott, Elsie's first husband's brother. Freddy Alcott used to live by Jean long before Jean and I met, and when we did first meet Jean she said that I was the spitting image of one of her customers at the shop where she worked on the estate - and that customer was Freddy, my dad may have been Freddy. It's quite a flamboyant name: Freddy Mills the boxer, Freddy Mercury the singer, Freddy Kruger, no let's not go there, let's just leave it at that till I am sure. In all seriousness, I am sure Geoff knew where I came from, hence the reason he befriended me as a child, I still don't know if either he or Joyce are alive or their kids either, maybe one day I will find out. On that point the mystery deepens. I don't need to hold back the tears anymore because I have released the pain of childhood and the hate and dislike that burned for so long, it has now gone, I feel washed clean, baptized by my own words, and realize that it's time to put all this to rest and try to be a better person.

Lastly, to all the part of my family that are gone, may they rest in peace: Elsie, Valerie, Dianne, Barry, Tommy - and now Joyce as I have just found out - the coincidental thing is, Marlene was taken ill at Christmas 2012 and Jean and I had to go and look after Arthur in his demented state whilst Marlene was in hospital, and who should turn up at the house from abroad but Marlene's son whom I had not seen for twenty-odd years, he happened to mention he had met Mike Kennedy in Amsterdam and obtained his phone number and coincidently Mike phoned him whilst he was in the U.K. to tell him Joyce had just died in an old folks' home, imagine my surprise.

It's now 4th March 2012, the sad news is that Marlene is at this moment is lying on her death bed and has been given two days left to live, the illness she has is cancer, she left it, knew of it, and never told anyone till the last week, she complained for many years of the pain that has now taken over her whole body, she lies in a dream state, a sort of coma induced by morphine. Whilst searching on a lonesome day amongst documents for Hans, her son, I found a letter from the girls, Ruth, Rita and Roberta, who still live in Australia and also a letter from Dennis, Joyce's first husband who is still alive in a home, maybe I may be fortunate enough to be able to write his life story and that of the kids, to be called *From the Wizard to Oz*, they were badly abused for fifteen years in that kids' home, it seems odd to me, often asking Marlene over the years, if she knew of them, which she denied. I was sitting up at ten to seven on the 7th of

March 2012, five to seven the phone rang, 'would you come to the hospital now because Marlene is drastically fading?' the noise awoke Jean who said she had just been dreaming of Marlene, in the dream Marlene sat up in a fluffy white bed, arms wide open and happy, with a blue shroud and a black tint to her hair and smiling, the phone rang again five minutes later, it was the hospital again, it was exactly seven o'clock. 'Sorry I went back to her room and she has died,' the nurse said, we both sat for a while in silence, the telly screen went blank, it just went silent, I checked everything and there was no reason for the problem, said to Jean, 'leave it it's probably the ghost in the machine I mentioned earlier in this book', we left the telly on and one hour later the screen flickered and the sound started to work though with broken speech similar to Marlene's. 'Okay Marlene, a joke's a joke,' I said, then the telly came on properly and all was fine, it was just Marlene letting us know she had passed into the stillness to await her fate.

Arthur is now permanently in that care home, all the goods and chattels of his past life sold to pay for his keep, to me it's a curse to have to live like that without memory of what was, a kind of prisoner not only of the mind but also of the body, is he carrying the burden of all his past deeds I ask myself. The wheel has turned full circle and soon he will face the final justice, maybe this is his last chance to repent and redeem himself before Judgement Day, I visit him regularly despite his past, and every time we speak I have to tell him Marlene is dead, to which he always shows sorrow, the remainder of his life will be like that. Just one last twist of fate, I received a telephone call from Holland three weeks after the death of Marlene, to tell me her son Hans had suddenly died at the age of sixty-seven, I'm glad it happened like that because none of them have had to suffer the great loss of death for a long period of time. So there you have it, the final chapter of my life so far complete, as seen from my point of view, never knowing anyone had any contact with the kids in Australia, I have now contacted Mike after fifty years and hope to start to re-join some of our long-lost family with the first piece of my new jigsaw, such is the power of a seventh-born.

By P. Davies

REPRISE

BE SURE THE PROMISES YOU MAKE. OUTWEIGH THE PROMISES YOU BREAK. THEN THE BALANCE OF JUSTICE WILL BE IN YOUR FAVOUR AND MAY YOUR GODS BLESS YOU ALL.

PEFC Certified

This product is
from sustainably
managed forests
and controlled
sources

www.pefc.org

PEFC/16-33-415